Pension Markets in Focus 2024

OECD
BETTER POLICIES FOR BETTER LIVES

Please cite this publication as:
OECD (2024), *Pension Markets in Focus 2024*, OECD Publishing, Paris, https://doi.org/10.1787/b11473d3-en.

ISBN 978-92-64-18199-1 (print)
ISBN 978-92-64-88016-0 (PDF)
ISBN 978-92-64-53836-8 (HTML)
ISBN 978-92-64-77843-6 (epub)

Pension Markets in Focus
ISSN 3006-8029 (print)
ISSN 3006-8037 (online)

Photo credits: Cover © grapestock/Adobe Stock.

Corrigenda to OECD publications may be found at: https://www.oecd.org/en/publications/support/corrigenda.html.

Foreword

Pension Markets in Focus provides detailed and comparable statistics on asset-backed pensions around the world. This publication aims to help policy makers, regulators and other stakeholders evaluate the design and operation of pension systems, and to support policy discussions through international comparisons. *Pension Markets in Focus* is published annually. A preliminary version is published in June based on initial data on selected variables, and the final version in the last quarter of the year based on the latest data on a more comprehensive set of variables.

The preliminary version of the 2024 edition of *Pension Markets in Focus* showed that assets earmarked for retirement grew in most jurisdictions in 2023. This growth contrasts with the large decline in assets in many OECD countries in 2022.

This final version of *Pension Markets in Focus 2024* explores whether the growth in assets earmarked for retirement was sufficient to offset the investment losses incurred in 2022, and how this growth in assets fits in the long-term trend. It first looks at the extent of the growth in assets in 2023 and the underlying drivers behind it. It then shows the jurisdictions in which the growth offset the losses incurred in 2022. It also compares the trends in 2023 with the long-term trends and examines whether the shift away from defined benefit plans to defined contribution plans continued.

Data used to prepare this report were collected from pension authorities and other bodies within the framework of the OECD's Global Pension Statistics project conducted under the aegis of the OECD Working Party on Private Pensions. The OECD's partnership with the International Organisation of Pension Supervisors (IOPS) and the World Bank expands the geographical coverage of the report beyond the OECD area. The OECD is grateful to the IOPS and the World Bank who helped with the data collection, and to pension authorities and other reporting bodies for providing data and comments.

The report was prepared by the Capital Markets and Financial Institutions Division within the OECD Directorate for Financial and Enterprise Affairs (DAF) and under the direction of Pablo Antolin, Head of the Division's Insurance and Pensions Unit. This report was prepared by Romain Despalins with insights and inputs from the Unit, in particular from Stéphanie Payet. Sally Day-Hanotiaux provided statistical assistance and comments. Eva Abbott, Tom Dannequin, Liv Gudmundson and Flora Monsaingeon-Lavuri provided editorial assistance and prepared the report for publication.

Table of contents

FIGURES

TABLES

Executive summary

This edition of Pension Markets in Focus explores whether the growth in assets earmarked for retirement in 2023 was sufficient to offset the investment losses incurred in 2022, and how this growth fits within the long-term trend. It looks at the extent of the growth of assets and the underlying drivers behind it, compares the trends in 2023 with the long-term trends and examines whether the shift away from defined benefit plans to defined contribution plans continued.

Assets earmarked for retirement grew by 10% in 2023 in the OECD

Assets earmarked for retirement grew by 10% in 2023 in nominal terms in the OECD, reaching USD 63.1 trillion by year-end. This growth resulted from the investment income that pension providers and public pension reserve funds earned following positive developments in equity markets. Positive cashflows from contributions over benefit payments and other expenditure also supported asset growth.

However, assets were not back to their 2021 level by end-2023 in the OECD

Assets earmarked for retirement in 2023 were still 5% below their 2021 level in nominal terms in the OECD area, despite asset growth in 2023. Pension providers and public pension reserve funds incurred large investment losses in 2022 following the rise in interest rates and falling equity valuations. Pension providers in the United States and some large pension markets in Europe had not recouped their investment losses by end-2023, driving the trend in the OECD area. This contrasts with most other, and generally smaller, pension markets where assets of pension providers exceeded their 2021 level by end-2023, as they recouped smaller investment losses faster and benefitted from the excess of contributions over benefit payments and other expenditure. Assets in OECD public pension reserve funds were also above their 2021 level except in a few countries, including the United States that has the largest public pension reserve fund in the OECD. The United States has been drawing down its reserves since 2021 to pay benefits.

The growth in assets in 2023 marks a return to the long-term trend of asset growth

The growth in assets in 2023 is consistent with the long-term trend of retirement asset growth despite episodes of decline such as during the 2008 financial crisis and COVID-19 pandemic. Assets more than tripled over the last two decades in the OECD, from USD 20.8 trillion at end-2003 to USD 63.1 trillion at end-2023 in current prices. This long-term trend partly results from the positive investment income that pension providers and public pension reserve funds have earned. It is also the result of the measures that governments have put in place to foster retirement savings, increase participation in and contributions to pension plans, and bolster reserves for public pay-as-you-go pension plans.

The long-term shift away from defined benefit plans continued

The solvency of defined benefit plans continued to improve in 2023, as the growth in assets outpaced the growth in liabilities. The ratio of assets over the liabilities of these plans (i.e. funding ratio) reached a record high in the United Kingdom and the United States, although it remained below 100% in the United States. The positive performance of equity markets offset the decline in discount rates towards the end of 2023, leading to higher funding ratios. Yet, the shift away from defined benefit towards defined contribution plans continued as some employers may have taken advantage of improving funding ratios to wind up plans and offload the risks and liabilities.

1 Assets earmarked for retirement grew in 2023

This section shows the amount and evolution of assets earmarked for retirement in 2023 and explores the drivers behind the developments.

The future provision of retirement benefits will depend on the amount of assets earmarked for retirement. Individuals can accrue assets or rights, backed by assets, through pension plans that they have access to through employment or on their own initiative. These assets accumulate in specific vehicles, such as pension funds, that financial institutions (hereafter, 'pension providers') administer.[1] Most OECD countries have also set up reserves to support benefit payments of the public pay-as-you-go (PAYG) pension system. These reserves also constitute assets earmarked for retirement that can be ring-fenced in a fund (hereafter, 'public pension reserve fund').

This section aims to assess the amount and evolution of assets earmarked for retirement in 2023 and to understand the drivers behind the developments during the year.

The section covers all asset-backed pension arrangements where assets accumulate to finance future retirement income, whether pension providers (private and public-sponsored) or public pension reserve funds invest these assets. The section covers pension providers from OECD countries and other jurisdictions participating in the OECD Global Pension Statistics project. The information on public pension reserve funds covers only OECD countries.[2]

The section is structured as follows. First, it presents the amount and evolution of assets earmarked for retirement in 2023. Then, it shows that the growth in assets partly resulted from a positive investment performance. Finally, it shows that the growth in assets was also the result of positive cashflows from contributions over benefit payments and other expenditure.

1.1. Assets earmarked for retirement reached USD 63.1 trillion in the OECD at end-2023

OECD countries had USD 63.1 trillion of assets earmarked for retirement at end-2023. This is 10% more than at end-2022 in current USD terms. Assets of both pension providers and public pension reserve funds increased in 2023 (Figure 1.1) but most of the growth was in plans managed by pension providers.

Figure 1.1. Assets earmarked for retirement in the OECD

In USD trillion

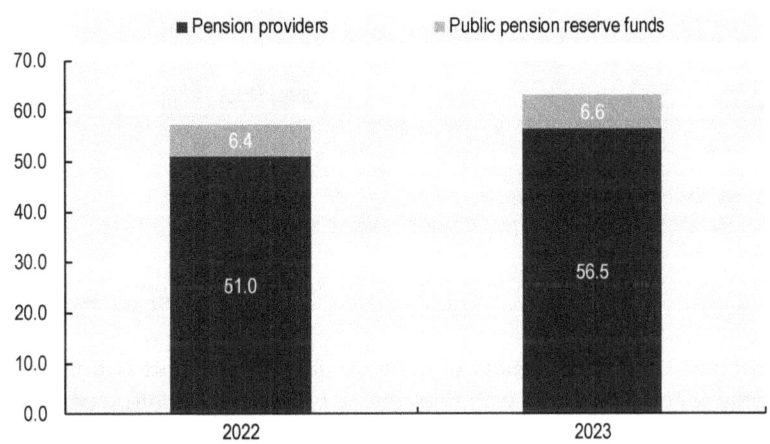

Note: For more details, please see the methodological notes in Annex C.
Source: OECD Global Pension Statistics.

StatLink https://stat.link/d1z9l6

Assets earmarked for retirement grew in 2023 in nearly all OECD countries, except Luxembourg and Portugal. Figure 1.2 shows the growth in assets by country in national currency and in nominal terms.[3] One explanation for the decline in these two countries is the closing of some plans and the transfer of assets. Two occupational funds were liquidated in Luxembourg in 2023. In Portugal, assets managed by a pension fund were transferred to the public pension system. OECD countries also held more reserves for their public PAYG systems, except the United States, which drew on its reserves in 2023 to pay benefits.

Figure 1.2. Nominal growth rates of assets earmarked for retirement in selected OECD countries, 2023

In per cent

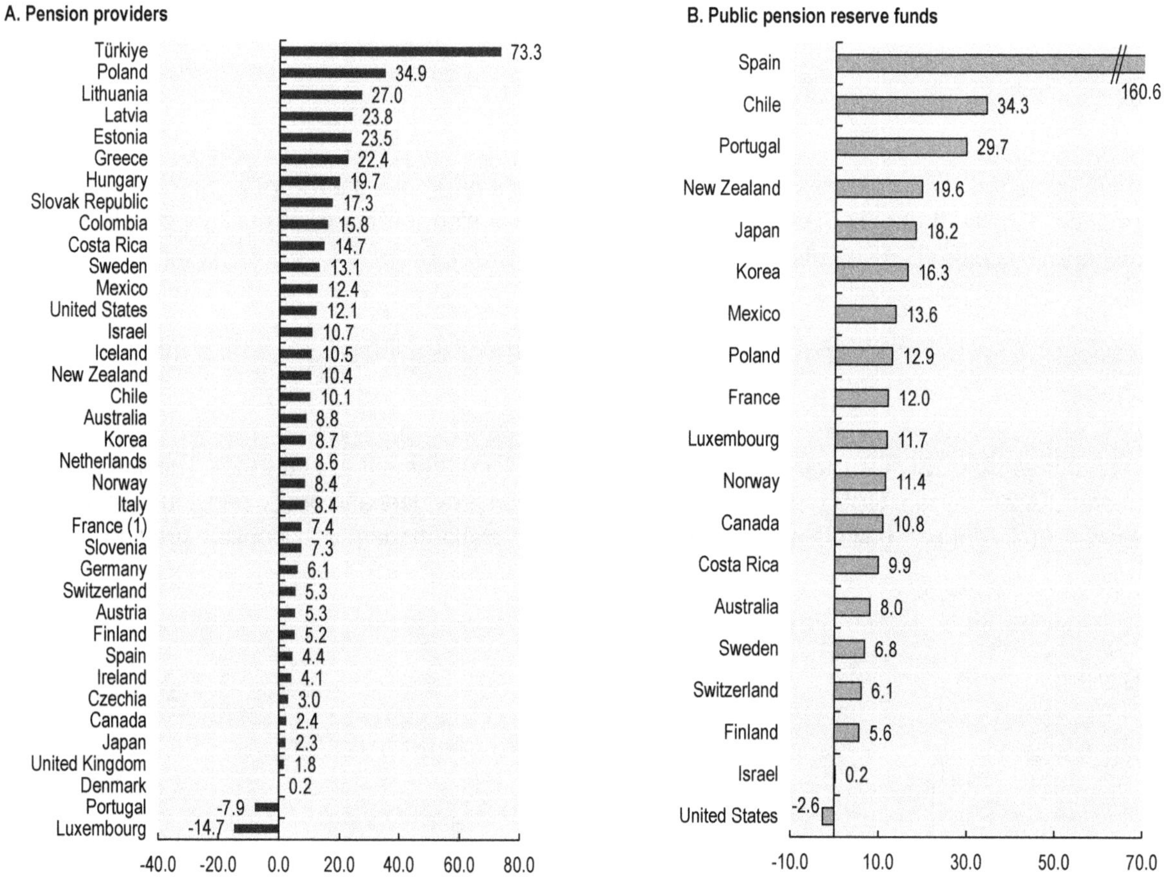

Note: For more details, please see the methodological notes in Annex C.
Source: OECD Global Pension Statistics and websites of public pension reserve funds.

StatLink https://stat.link/jg69na

There are large differences in terms of assets of pension providers across countries. Countries with the largest amount of assets tend to be those with mandatory or quasi-mandatory pension arrangements. In Iceland and Switzerland, where employers must provide an occupational plan to their employees, pension providers held assets worth 182% and 160% of GDP, respectively (Figure 1.3).[4] In Denmark and the Netherlands where employers must participate in a pension plan when agreed upon at the industry or branch level, the amount of assets is also high relative to GDP. Countries with voluntary or more recent pension arrangements had lower pools of assets, with some notable exceptions such as the United States. In the United States, where people have been saving for retirement for several decades, pension providers held assets worth USD 39 trillion, representing nearly 70% of all assets held by pension providers in the OECD area. In other countries with voluntary or recently introduced pension arrangements such as Greece, Hungary and Türkiye, assets earmarked for retirement are still limited.

Figure 1.3. Assets of pension providers and public pension reserve funds in selected OECD countries at end-2023

As a % of GDP and in USD billion

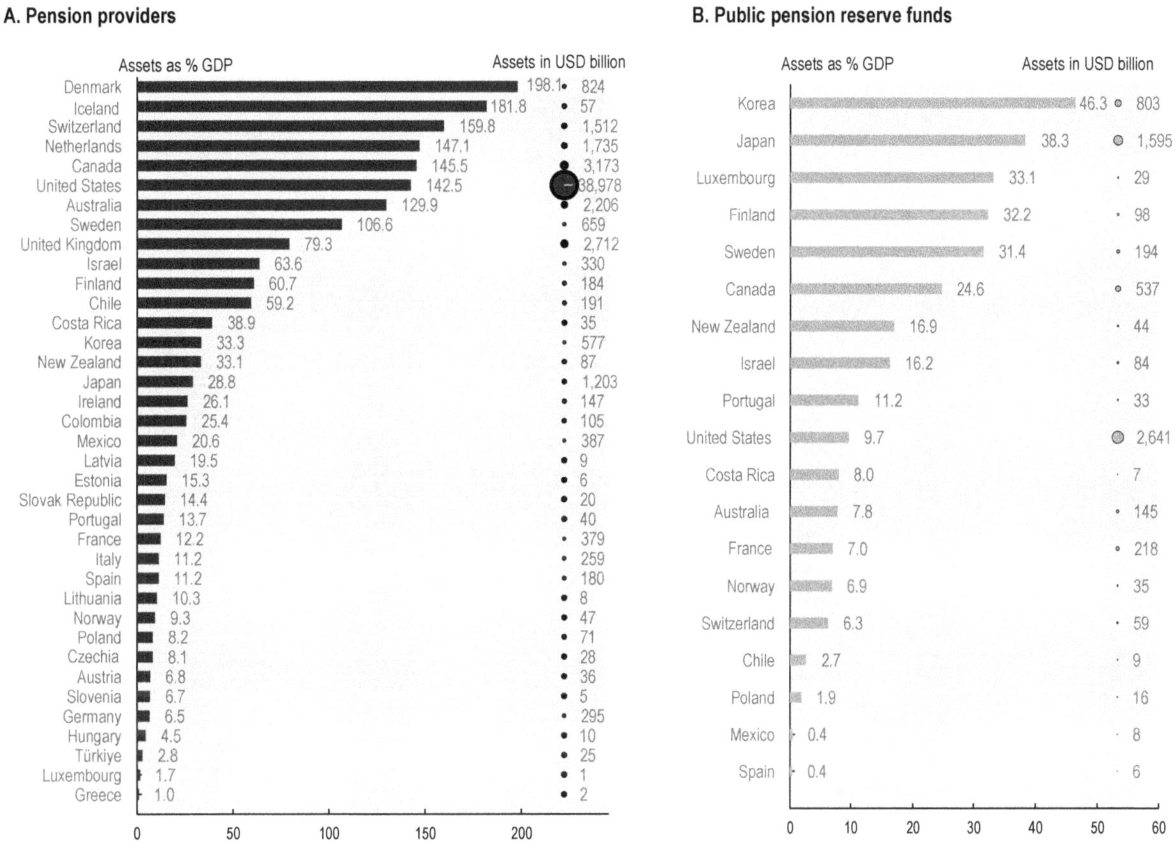

Note: For more details, please see the methodological notes in Annex C.
Source: OECD Global Pension Statistics and websites of public pension reserve funds.

StatLink https://stat.link/rw28z3

The size of the reserves of the public PAYG system also varies widely across countries. The United States still had the largest public pension reserve fund in the OECD in 2023 with USD 2.6 trillion in reserves, despite the decline in reserves during the year. Korea and Japan had the largest amounts of reserves of PAYG schemes relative to the size of their economy (at 46% and 38% of GDP respectively). By contrast, Spain had the lowest reserves (both in USD and as % of GDP) among those countries reporting in Figure 1.3. The reasons for the differences in the size of reserves could include the date of introduction of the reserve fund, its mission, any limit or target in size, and depletion date.[5]

Assets earmarked for retirement also grew in non-OECD jurisdictions in 2023, in several cases faster than in most OECD countries. Growth was the strongest in jurisdictions with recent mandatory pension arrangements (e.g. Armenia, Georgia, Ghana, Malawi) (Figure 1.4). Yet, the importance of asset-backed pensions was still limited and non-OECD jurisdictions had a lower amount of assets in absolute terms and as a percentage of GDP than OECD countries with the largest pools (Figure 1.5).[6]

Figure 1.4. Nominal growth rates of assets of pension providers outside the OECD, 2023

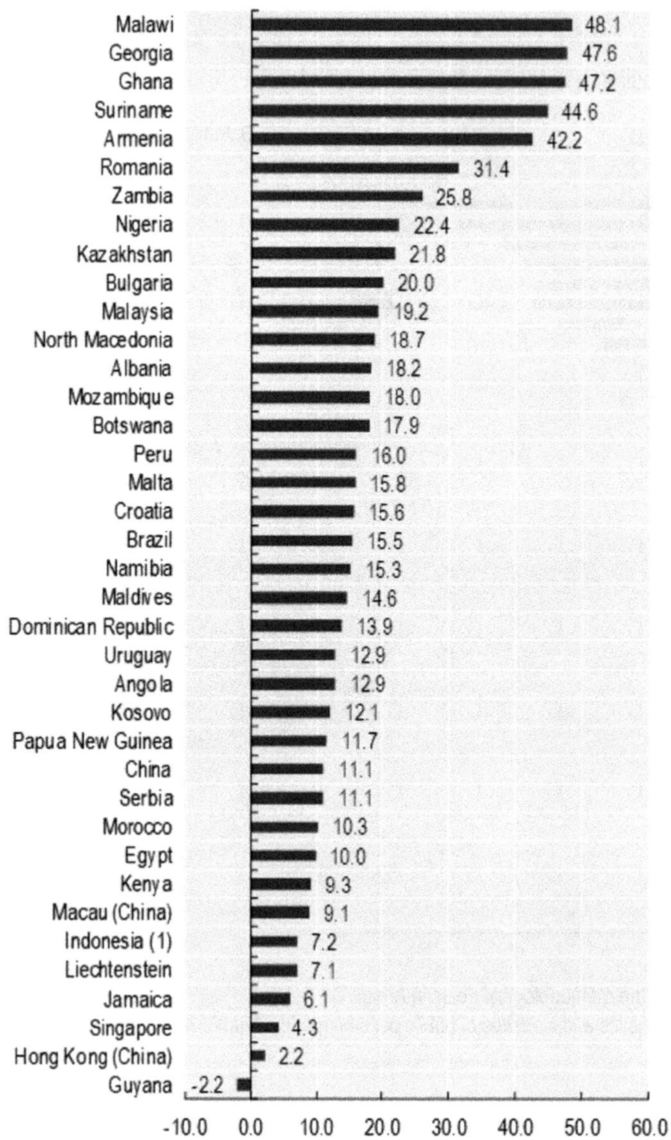

Note: For more details, please see the methodological notes in Annex C.
Source: OECD Global Pension Statistics.

StatLink https://stat.link/nsyo8q

Figure 1.5. Assets of pension providers in selected non-OECD jurisdictions at end-2023

As a % of GDP and in USD billion

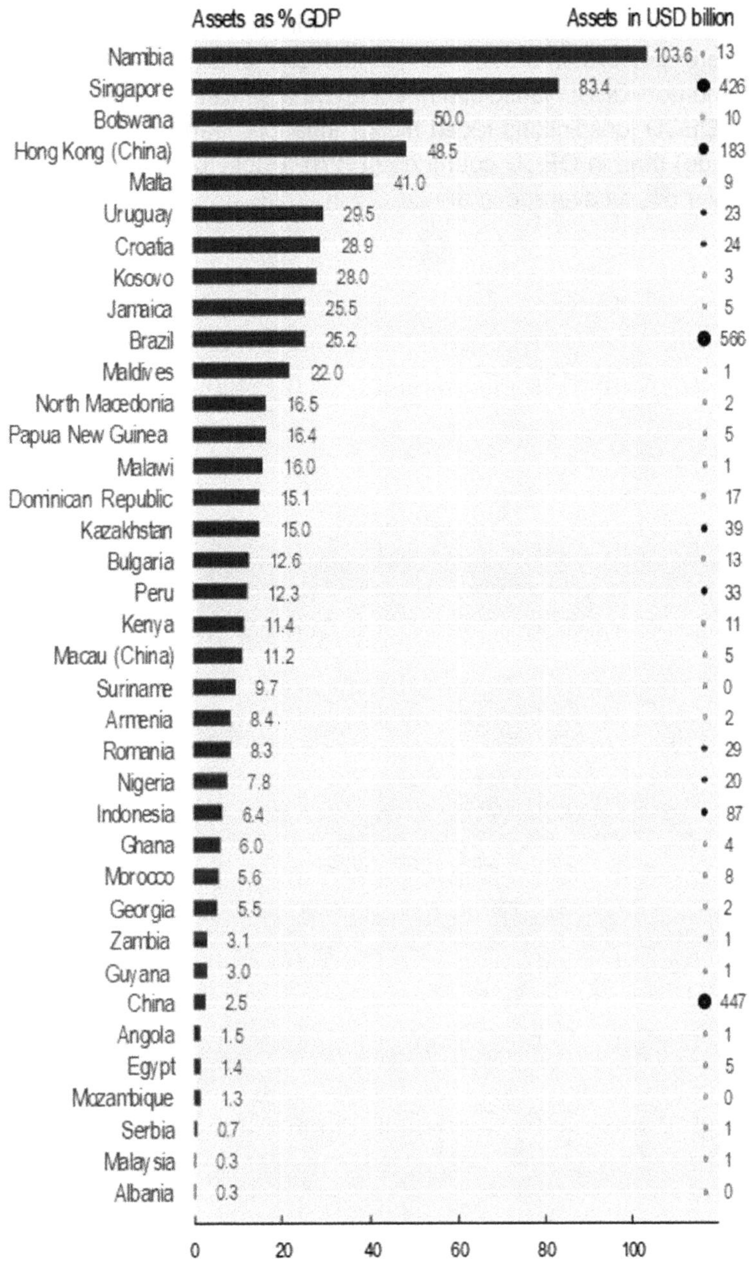

Note: For more details, please see the methodological notes in Annex C.
Source: OECD Global Pension Statistics.

StatLink https://stat.link/z3xl7o

1.2. The growth in assets partly resulted from a positive investment performance

The growth in assets in 2023 partly resulted from the positive investment performance that pension providers and public pension reserve funds achieved during the year. The nominal rates of return of pension providers were positive in nearly all jurisdictions and exceeded inflation in most of them (Figure 1.6). OECD and non-OECD jurisdictions achieved a similar nominal rate of return on average (at 10%). However, non-OECD jurisdictions faced higher inflation, leading to lower real investment rates of return (1.5% on average) than in OECD countries (4.8%). Public pension reserve funds recorded a real rate of return of just over 5% on average in the OECD in 2023.

Figure 1.6. Nominal and real investment rates of return of asset-backed pension systems in 2023

In per cent

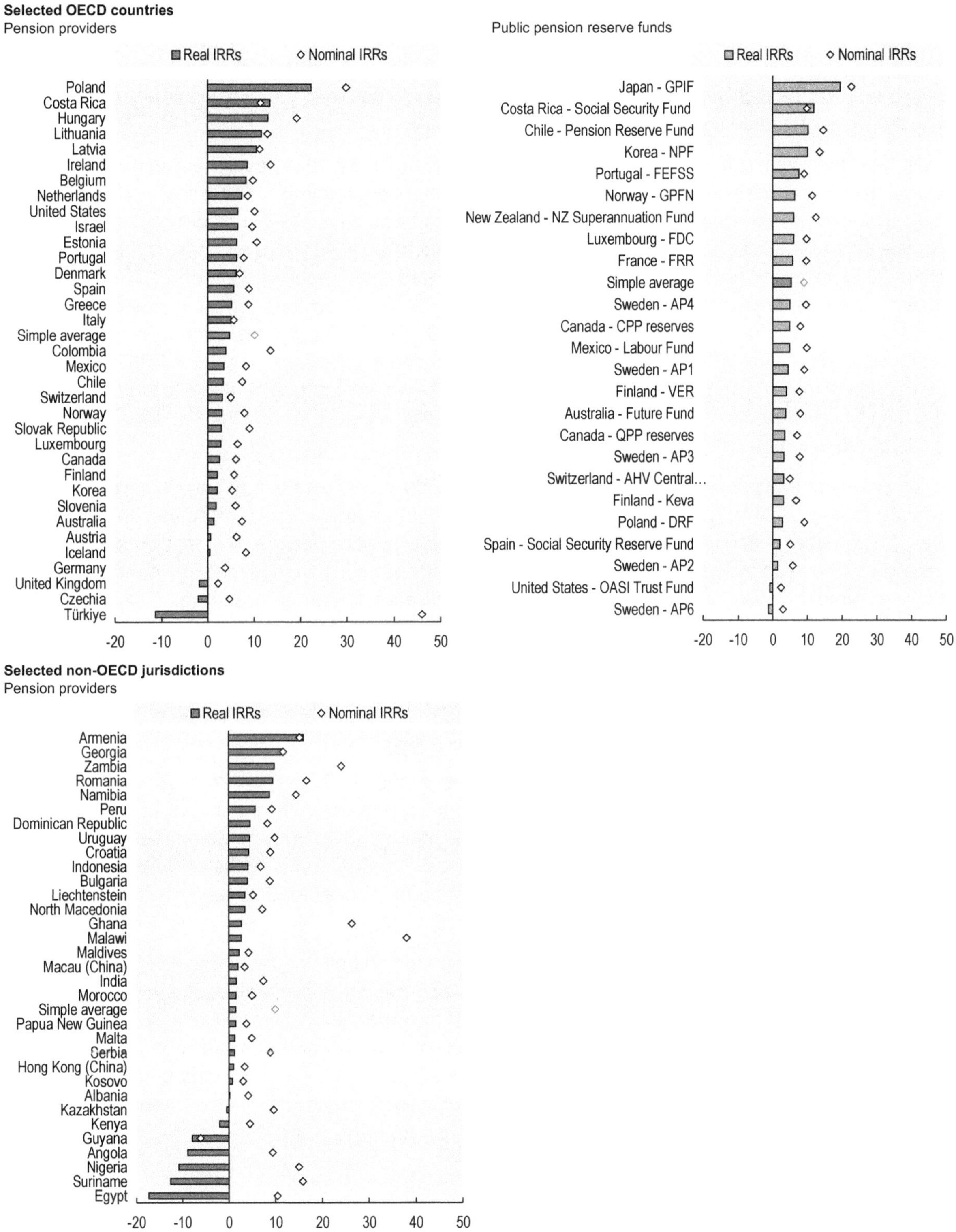

Note: For more details, please see the methodological notes in Annex C.
Source: OECD Global Pension Statistics and other sources.

StatLink https://stat.link/wcuzlm

This strong investment performance was the result of positive developments in equity markets in 2023. The MSCI World Index rose by 20% in 2023.[7] Equity prices globally rose as inflation pressures eased and investors expected interest rate cuts. Positive developments in equity markets generally favoured those investing the most in equities, such as pension providers in Latvia, Lithuania and Poland (Figure 1.7). Yet, some equity markets underperformed in 2023, including Hong Kong (China) (SFC, 2024[1]) and the People's Republic of China (hereafter 'China') because of the downturn in the property market (IMF, 2024[2]). Jurisdictions highly exposed to equity markets would experience lower investment performance when equity markets underperform (e.g. Hong Kong (China)).

The yields on long-term government bonds reversed course in 2023 in many countries, improving pension providers' return on these instruments. Bonds are the main instrument in which pension providers and public pension reserve funds invest. A rise in yields leads to losses on bonds issued previously with a lower yield, and conversely. While yields on long-term government bonds increased and reached a peak in October 2023 in major advanced economies, they declined in the last quarter of 2023 as investors expected cuts in interest rates (BIS, 2024[3]; IMF, 2024[2]). Yields on long-term government bonds in emerging market economies also fell at the end of 2023 (BIS, 2024[3]). This decline in the yields on government bonds benefited pension providers and public pension reserve funds in Q4 2023 when they valued bonds on a mark-to-market basis. The valuation method is important as those using an amortised cost method (e.g. based on effective interest rates) are less sensitive to changes in government bond yields (e.g. Albania, Poland's Demographic Reserve Fund).

Pension providers and public pension reserve funds investing in real estate may have incurred losses on this asset class in 2023. High inflation and the rise of interest rates adversely impacted commercial real estate.[8] The number of transactions declined because of the difference between the price sought by sellers for their properties and the price potential buyers were ready to pay.[9] Changes in working habits with an increase in remote working also led to vacancies in the office sector and a fall in rents,[10] causing further losses for real estate. These developments weighted on the investment performance of pension funds in Australia and Canada (which held 15% and 11% of their assets in land and buildings), for example. Sweden's AP Funds 1 to 4 also suffered losses in their real estate investments which account for around 15% of their portfolio. Sweden's AP Funds 1 to 4 managed to offset these losses through gains on other asset classes, in particular equities, to achieve an overall positive return in 2023.

The funds that experienced the lowest returns in 2023 were those that could not reap benefits from listed equities. The mandate of Sweden's AP6 fund is to invest in the private equity market (i.e. unlisted equities) (AP6, 2024[4]). AP6 held 0.1% of its assets in listed equities and 93.9% in unlisted equities at end-2023, achieving one of the lowest performances in 2023 compared to other funds. Pension funds in the Czech Republic (hereafter 'Czechia') also had one of the lowest performances in 2023 as a result of having one of the lowest shares of assets invested in equities.

For those investing heavily abroad, investment gains depended on both the performance of foreign assets and the exchange rates between the domestic currency and the currency these assets were issued in.[11] Pension funds in Chile and Colombia invest 45% of their portfolio abroad. Chile recorded foreign investment gains in 2023, reinforced by the depreciation of the Chilean peso against the main foreign currencies, such as the US dollar. By contrast, Colombia experienced one of the strongest appreciations of its currency against the US dollar in 2023.[12] This revaluation lowered the gains of Colombian pension funds on foreign investments in 2023.

Figure 1.7. Allocation of assets earmarked for retirement in selected asset classes and investment vehicles, at end-2023

As a percentage of total investment

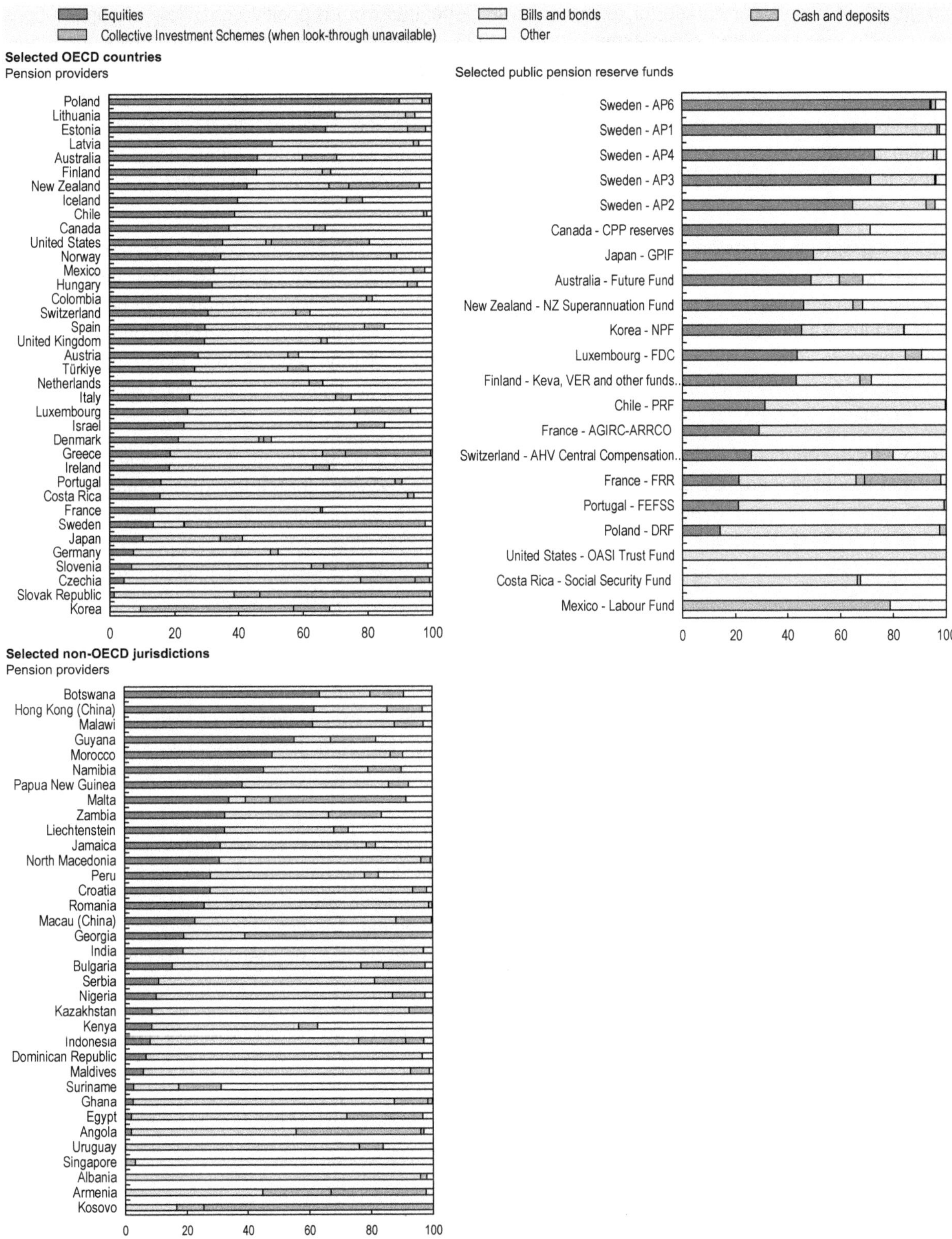

Note: For more details, please see the methodological notes in Annex C.
Source: OECD Global Pension Statistics and other sources.

StatLink https://stat.link/i10b8r

1.3. Positive cashflows from contributions over expenditure also contributed to the growth of assets in 2023

The growth in assets earmarked for retirement also benefitted from a positive cashflow of contributions over benefit payments and other expenditure in 2023. Figure 1.8 shows that most pension providers recorded an excess of contributions over benefit payments and other expenditure. Contributions for pension providers came from employers, individuals or governments through state matching contributions (e.g. New Zealand, Türkiye) or fixed nominal subsidies (e.g. Poland, Türkiye) (OECD, 2023[5]). Outflows of pension providers include retirement benefits (e.g. lump sum, programmed withdrawals, annuity) paid directly to retirees or through transfers to other institutions in charge of the pay-out phase; early withdrawals when allowed; and operating expenses.

The demographics of pension plan members are key to understanding the cash flows of pension providers. In 2023, positive cashflows were larger in jurisdictions that recently introduced or expanded their pension arrangements and mandated participation (e.g. Armenia, Greece, Georgia). Contributions were higher than benefit payments as these plans were gaining new members and usually had not started or only just started paying benefits. This contrasts with more mature systems that pay benefits to a larger proportion of members. Benefit payments of pension providers exceeded contributions they received in Canada, Finland and the United Kingdom, for instance.[13]

Strong employment and wage growth supported pension contributions in 2023. Employment rates improved modestly in the OECD and globally in 2023 (OECD, 2024[6]; ILO, 2024[7]), with many countries recording historically high levels of employment. High and increasing employment rates mean that a larger proportion of the working-age population can access a pension plan through work when available. Real wages grew by 3.5% on average between Q1 2023 and Q1 2024 in the OECD. Lithuania, which has one of the largest excess of contributions over expenditure, is one of the OECD countries where real wages increased the most between Q1 2023 and Q1 2024 (by 4.9%). The rise in wages automatically increases contributions to pension plans when they are levied as a percentage of salary, other things being equal. In Australia, the increase in contribution rates further boosted contribution inflows in 2023.[14]

One challenge that some countries experienced, especially in Africa, was to ensure that employers remitted their mandatory contributions. For example, Malawi reported that contribution arrears grew as some employers failed to remit pension contributions. In Nigeria, rising inflation contributed to a decline in the remittance of contributions, which lowered asset growth.

Early withdrawals and transfers of money out of a plan can drain the assets of pension providers. Early withdrawals and transfers represent an outflow, or leakage, for the asset-backed pension system as a whole, unless the amount withdrawn or transferred is put back into another pension arrangement. Individuals directly receive money from pension providers when they withdraw their assets, and this money is unlikely to return to the asset-backed pension system. Transfers may happen when individuals change fund, change job and roll over the assets, reach retirement age and receive payments from a different institution, or when funds wind up - on their initiative or urged by national authorities - or purchase buy-out contracts. Assets remain in the system until they are paid to individuals.

Figure 1.8. Excess of contributions to pension providers over expenditure in 2023

As a % of assets at end-2022

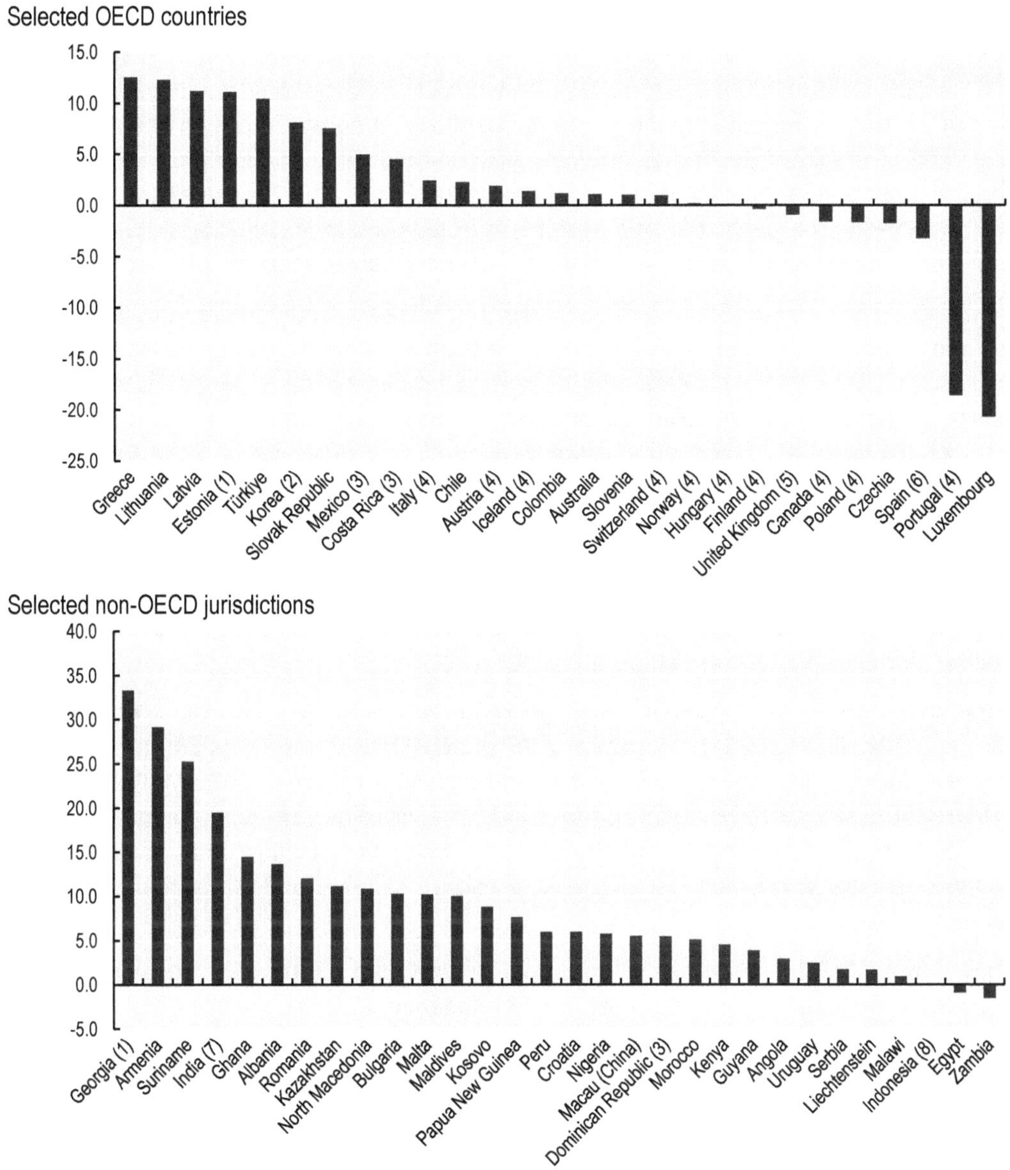

Note: The excess of contributions over expenditure is calculated as the difference between the change in assets between end-2022 and end-2023 and the investment income (net of investment expenses) earned during 2023. It is expressed as a percentage of assets at end-2022. Expenditure includes benefit payments to retirees, early withdrawals, administrative expenses and other operating expenses, and transfers out of the system. For more details, see the methodological notes in Annex C.
Source: OECD Global Pension Statistics.

StatLink https://stat.link/4stvqy

In 2023, pension providers recorded larger outflows from early withdrawals in Costa Rica and some African countries. Many countries allow people to access their savings before retirement and set the conditions that plan members need to fulfil to be able to access the savings, the purchase of a home being the most common one (OECD, 2019[8]). In Costa Rica, more people accessed their savings from voluntary pension funds in 2023 than in 2022 following an increase in the early retirement age at which people can get their public pension, effective from 2024.[15] Some African countries relaxed the conditions to access savings in 2023. Zambia allowed a one-off partial withdrawal of 20% of assets by eligible members,[16] which may explain the negative cash flows of pension providers in 2023. In Malawi, a new law allows members close to retirement age to access up to 50% of their assets as a lump sum and reduces the waiting period for early withdrawals upon termination of employment. This easier access to savings may explain the small positive cashflow in Malawi.

The winding up of funds contributed to the negative cashflows in some European countries in 2023. Two occupational funds were liquidated in Luxembourg, with one merging with another fund based in another country and the other one terminating because of cost issues. In Portugal, assets managed by a pension fund were transferred to the public pension system. In Ireland, many occupational funds are winding up but most are transferring to another one and remain within the pension landscape.

The nature of the inflows and outflows from public pension reserve funds differs from those from pension providers. In most cases, revenues from public pension reserve funds come from the surplus of contributions to the public PAYG scheme over benefit payments and other expenditure (OECD, 2021[9]). Public pension reserve funds can also be financed through revenues from privatisation, earmarked contributions or tax, special or one-off contributions, and any other fiscal transfer (OECD, 2021[9]). Withdrawals from public pension reserve funds depend on certain conditions established in their mandates. Funds that build up a part of their assets from the excess of contributions over benefit payments in PAYG plans often experience a drawdown of their assets when commitments start exceeding inflows, as reserve funds are expected to make up the difference. In cases where reserves are mainly financed through budget transfers or are intended to support non-contributory pension plans, the law usually stipulates the circumstances or dates when assets can be used.

The balance of public PAYG systems meant only certain countries benefited from an excess of contributions over benefits in 2023. The balance of the public PAYG system was positive in Canada, Korea and Switzerland, for instance (Figure 1.9). Switzerland passed a reform in 2022 (AHV21) - in effect from 2024 - to maintain this positive balance and to secure the financing of public pensions until 2030. By contrast, Finland, Sweden and the United States had a negative cashflow from contributions from the PAYG system over benefit payments. These countries had to take funds from their reserves to cover benefit payments.

The cashflows of public pension reserve funds that are not tied to the balance of the PAYG system depended on the conditions to fill up the reserves. For instance, in Chile, the contributions to the reserve fund depend on the fiscal surplus. Inflows to the fund in 2023 were the maximum allowed by law. In France, since 2010 the *Fonds de réserve pour les retraites* (FRR) no longer receives any income other than its earnings from financial markets. The cash flow of the FRR was negative in 2023 as it had to pay EUR 2.1 billion to the *Caisse d'Amortissement de la dette sociale* (CADES) (FRR, Annual Report 2023[10]).[17]

Some countries, such as Spain, decided to bolster their public pension reserve fund. Spain had nearly depleted its reserves and decided to replenish them in 2023 by transferring the surplus of the mutual insurance companies and the Intergenerational Equity Mechanism (Ministry for Inclusion, Social Security and Migration, 2024[11]).

Figure 1.9. Differences between inflows and outflows of selected public pension reserve funds

As a % of assets at end-2022

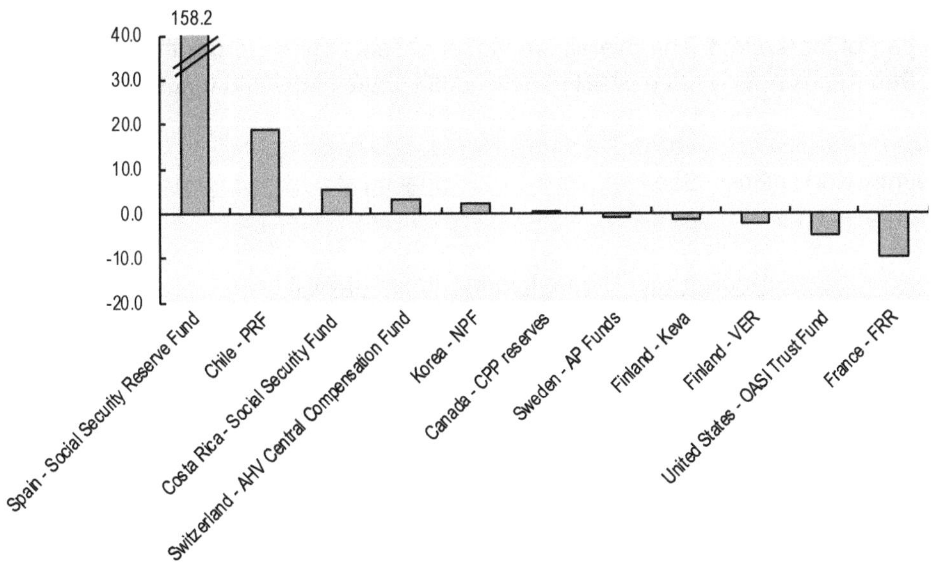

Source: OECD Global Pension Statistics and websites of public pension reserve funds.

StatLink https://stat.link/yrz35q

Notes

[1] See Annex A for more details.

[2] Data on public pension reserve funds come from their websites and from the inputs of the participants in the OECD Global Pension Statistics project.

[3] Assets also grew in nearly all OECD countries in USD terms. Israel and Japan are the only countries where assets of pension providers (for Japan) or in a public pension reserve fund (for Israel) increased in national currency but decreased in USD. This difference is due to the depreciation of the shekel and yen against the US dollar in 2023.

[4] Figure 1.3 shows data based on the OECD Global Pension Statistics exercise. Data for some jurisdictions only cover a part of the system. The overall amount of assets may be larger than in Figure 1.3 for some jurisdictions. See Annex A for a more detailed description of the plans and funds covered in this report, by jurisdiction.

[5] For example, Germany's Sustainability Fund is a short-term liquidity fund that should cover between 0.2 and 1.5 month of public pension payments. Reserves in this fund amounted to 1.1% of GDP at end-2022

(2023 data not available at the time of the drafting of this report). See (OECD, 2021[9]) for more details on the different types and features of public pension reserve funds.

[6] Figure 1.5 shows data based on the OECD Global Pension Statistics exercise. Data for some jurisdictions only cover a part of the system. The overall amount of assets may be larger than in Figure 1.5 for some jurisdictions. See Annex A for a more detailed description of the plans and funds covered in this report, by jurisdiction.

[7] MSCI all-country world stocks. See Markets in 2023: Soaring stocks and roaring bonds defy the doubters | Reuters

[8] Real Assets in Focus: Grappling with Higher Interest Rates - MSCI

[9] 2024 Trends to Watch in Real Assets - MSCI

[10] Real Assets in Focus: Grappling with Higher Interest Rates - MSCI

[11] See Annex B for the time series of the share of assets of pension providers invested abroad.

[12] Markets in 2023: Soaring stocks and roaring bonds defy the doubters | Reuters

[13] See Annex B for time series of contributions and benefit payments as % of GDP.

[14] The mandatory contribution rate for employers increased from 10.5% to 11% of salary in July 2023.

[15] From 2024, men can only receive a pension once they reach 65 (the statutory retirement age) instead of 62. Women can only receive a pension without penalty two years before the statutory retirement age, i.e. from age 63 instead of 59 years and 11 months (OECD, 2023[22])

[16] Members could withdraw up to 20% of their assets when they have contributed for at least five years. See PMRC BLOG

[17] The mission of the Caisse d'Amortissement de la Dette Sociale (CADES) is to fund and redeem the debt of the French Social Security.

2 Assets were not back to their 2021 level at end-2023 in the OECD area

This section shows that asset-backed pension systems have not recovered the losses they suffered in 2022 and the level of assets in 2023 is not back to their 2021 level.

This section aims to explore whether asset-backed pension systems had recovered the losses in 2022 and seen assets back to their 2021 level. The growth in assets in 2023 contrasts with its decline observed in 2022. The rise in interest rates in 2022 and falling equity valuations led to widespread investment losses in 2022 (OECD, 2023[12]). These losses led to a drop in the amount of assets earmarked for retirement, unseen since the 2008 financial crisis in most OECD countries.

Assets in 2023 were below their 2021 level in the OECD area. This decline was driven by the United States and other large European markets (e.g. Netherlands, United Kingdom) where pension providers have not recouped their investment losses from 2022. However, assets exceeded their 2021 level in most other jurisdictions as a result of investments gains and positive cashflows. In the case of public pension reserve funds, the cashflow of the largest reserve fund in the OECD (the US OASI Trust Fund) has been negative as the United States has been drawing on the reserves, explaining the shortfall in 2023 compared to 2021 in the OECD area.

This section first shows how assets for retirement in 2023 compare with their 2021 level in the OECD area. It then identifies the countries where pension providers and public pension reserve funds have not yet recovered their investment losses from 2022. It finally explores the cashflows of pension providers and public pension reserve funds between end-2021 and end-2023.

2.1. Assets for retirement remained 5% below their 2021 level at end-2023 in the OECD

Assets earmarked for retirement at end-2023 remained 5% below their 2021 level in nominal terms in the OECD area. Assets of pension providers dropped from USD 59.7 trillion at end-2021 to USD 51 trillion at end-2022, as higher interest rates and falling equity valuations caused large investment losses among most pension providers (OECD, 2023[12]). The growth in assets in 2023 was insufficient to bring them back to their 2021 level in USD terms (USD 56.5 trillion at end-2023) (Figure 2.1). Likewise, assets in public pension reserve funds were down by 5% in nominal and USD terms compared to end-2021 (Figure 2.2).

Figure 2.1. Assets of pension providers in the OECD, 2021-2023

In USD billion

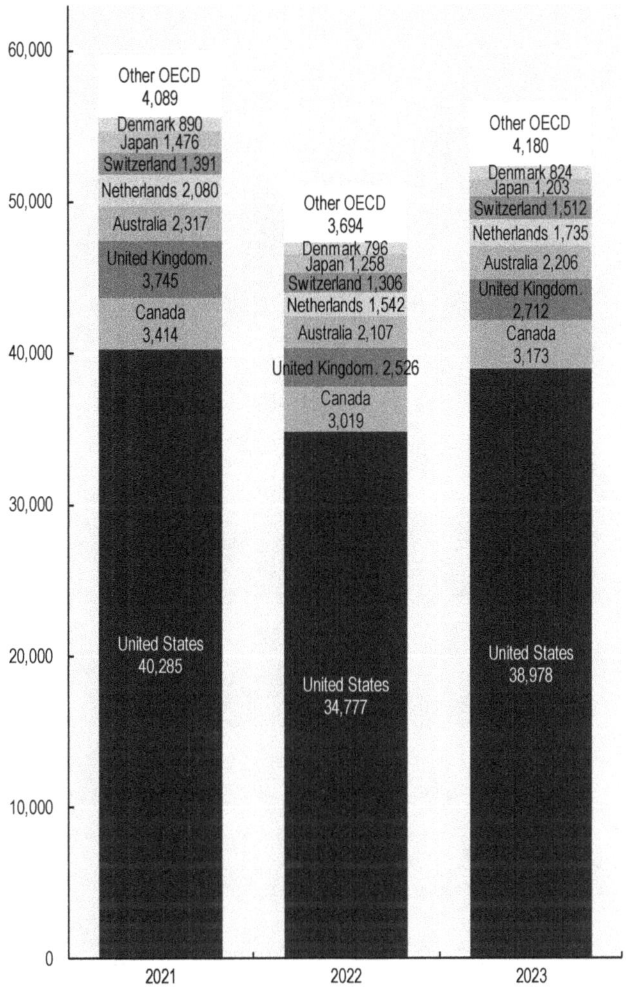

Note: For more details, please see the methodological notes in Annex C.
Source: OECD Global Pension Statistics.

StatLink https://stat.link/yk1mwp

Figure 2.2. Assets in OECD public pension reserve funds, 2021-2023

In USD billion

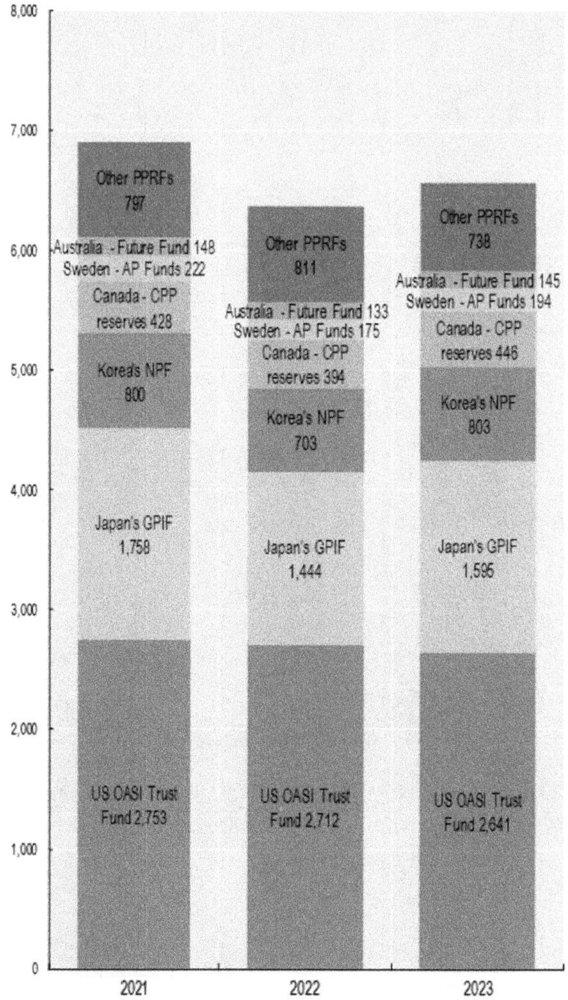

Note: For more details, please see the methodological notes in Annex C.
Source: OECD Global Pension Statistics and websites of public pension reserve funds.

StatLink https://stat.link/mge9nq

The largest markets accounted for the largest shortfalls in the level of assets in nominal and USD terms in the OECD between 2021 and 2023. The eight largest pension markets account for over 90% of assets of pension providers. Pension providers in these eight markets had fewer assets in USD terms at end-2023 than at end-2021, except in Switzerland. Some of the largest public pension reserve funds also had lower reserves at end-2023 than at end-2021, including Australia's Future Fund, Japan's GPIF, Sweden's AP Funds and the US OASI Trust Fund.

The lower level in assets in USD terms reflects changes in exchange rates between end-2021 and end-2023 in several countries. Assets decreased in USD terms but increased in national currency in some of the largest markets, including Australia and Japan (Figure 2.3). Similarly, the reserves of Australia's Future Fund and Japan's GPIF decreased in USD terms but increased in national currency. While the growth of Korea's National Pension Fund is small in USD terms (0.5%), it is more significant in national currency (9.2%). By contrast, assets of the reserve fund and pension providers in Switzerland increased in USD terms but were the same at end-2023 as at end-2021 in national currency because of the depreciation of the US dollar against the Swiss franc.

Figure 2.3. Per cent change of assets earmarked for retirement between end-2021 and end-2023 in selected OECD countries

A. Pension providers

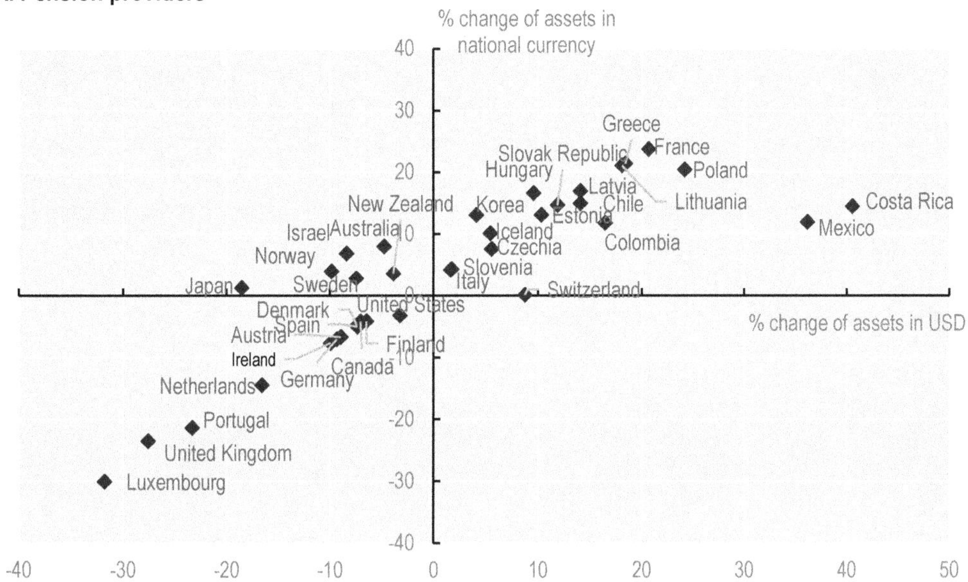

B. Public pension reserve funds

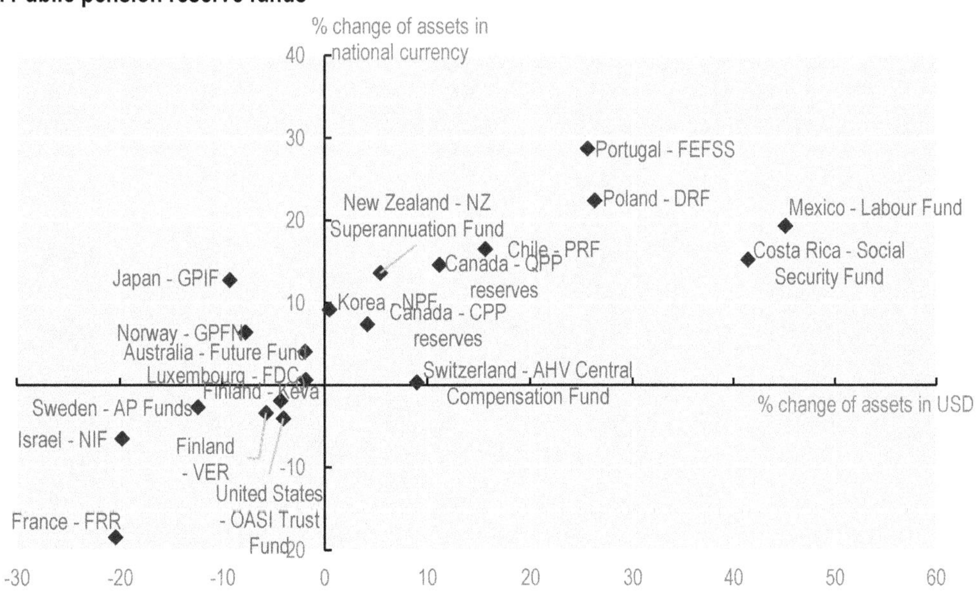

Note: For more details, please see the methodological notes in Annex C.
Source: OECD Global Pension Statistics and websites of public pension reserve funds.

StatLink https://stat.link/kue9yd

Assets at end-2023 were above their 2021 level in national currency in most countries but the largest ones. The evolution of assets in national currency is more important than in USD at the level of a given country as retirement benefits will be paid in national currency. Assets of pension providers were higher in national currency at end-2023 than at end-2021 in just over two thirds of OECD countries. Exceptions include some of the largest pension markets, in particular Denmark (-4.9%), the Netherlands (-14.5%), the United Kingdom (-23.6%) and the United States (-3.2%). Likewise, reserves of public pension reserve funds at end-2023 were above their 2021 level in national currency in most OECD countries, except in Finland, France (FRR), Israel, Sweden and the United States.

Countries with the largest decline in assets between end-2021 and end-2023 were those where assets declined both in 2022 and in 2023. While assets declined in most OECD countries in 2022, they continued to decline through 2023 in Luxembourg and Portugal (Figure 1.2), which both recorded some of the largest drops in assets (Figure 2.4). Countries where the growth in assets in 2023 was insufficient to offset the drop in 2022 include: Austria, Canada, Denmark, Finland, Germany, Ireland, the Netherlands, Spain, the United Kingdom and the United States. In the case of public pension reserve funds, reserves of France's FRR and the US OASI Trust Fund declined in 2022 and continued to do so in 2023. The increase in reserves was insufficient to offset the decline in 2022 in Finland, Israel and Sweden.

Figure 2.4. Level of assets earmarked for retirement relative to 2021

Reference: 2021 = 100

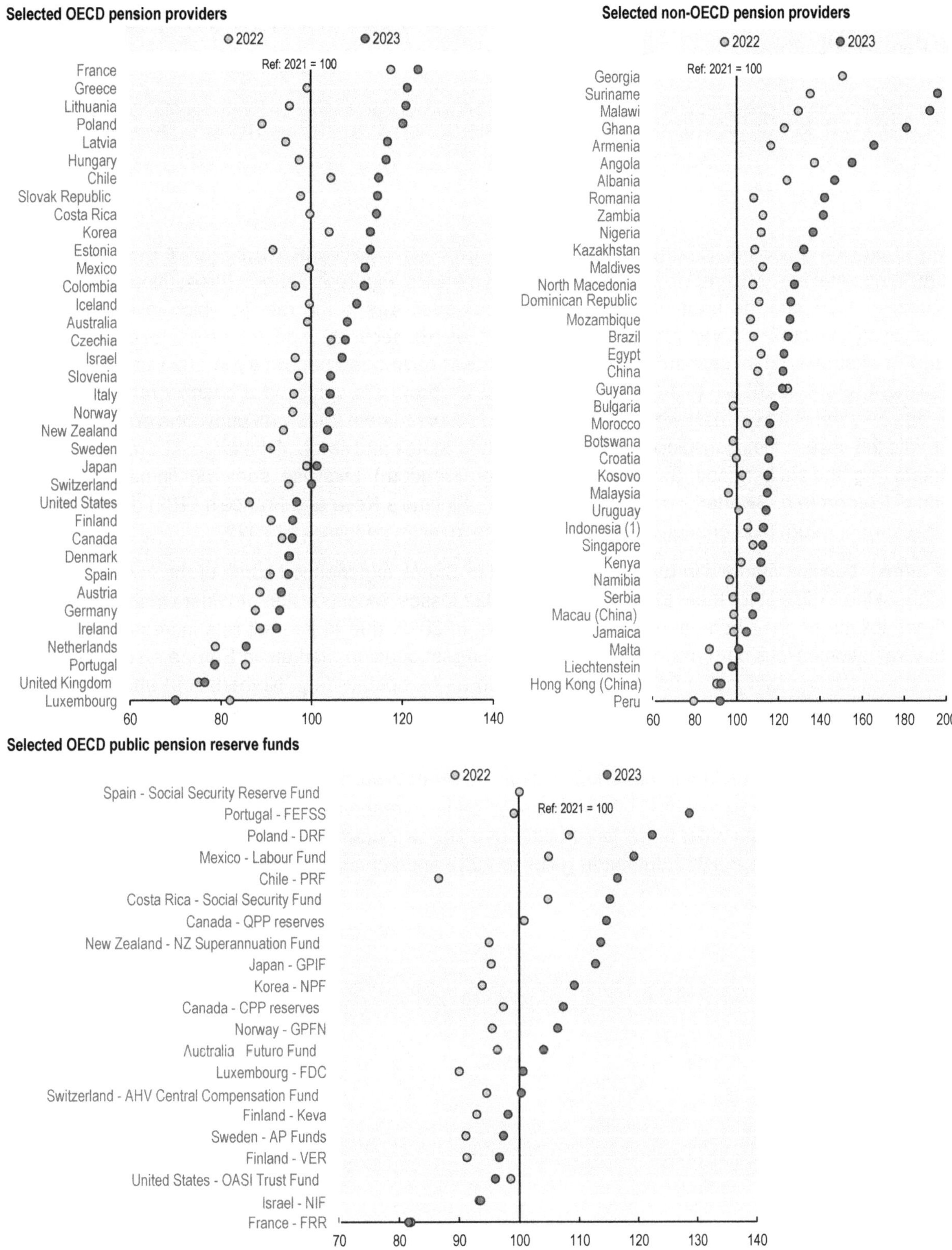

Note: For more details, please see the methodological notes in Annex C.

Source: OECD Global Pension Statistics and websites of public pension reserve funds.

StatLink https://stat.link/j4h3ui

Assets of pension providers were higher at end-2023 than at end-2021 more often outside the OECD area than in the OECD area. This is to some extent because the decline in assets in 2022 was less common for pension providers in non-OECD jurisdictions than in OECD countries. The only non-OECD jurisdictions where assets declined between 2021 and 2023 were Liechtenstein (-2.2%), Hong Kong (China) (-7.4%) and Peru (-7.9%).

2.2. Pension providers and public pension reserve funds achieved positive average investment rates of return over the last two years, except in some of the largest markets

Pension providers and public pension reserve funds achieved positive average returns over the last two years, in nominal terms, except in some of the largest markets. Figure 2.5 shows the nominal rate of return in 2022, in 2023 and the break-even rate. The break-even rate is the rate at which investment gains (respectively losses) in a given year fully offset the losses (respectively wipe out the gains) of the previous year. For example, an investment return of 11.1% would have been necessary in 2023 to offset a -10% investment return in 2022 (i.e. 1/(1+(-10%))-1). Pension providers achieved a positive rate of return on average over the last two years when the investment rate of return in 2023 was above the break-even rate. This was the case in most jurisdictions except the United States and some of the largest European pension markets (e.g. the Netherlands, Switzerland, the United Kingdom). Likewise, some public pension reserve funds in Europe (e.g. Sweden (except AP3 and AP6), Finland's Keva and France's FRR) did not achieve an investment return high enough in 2023 to offset the investment losses of 2022.

The largest pension markets in Europe and the United States experienced some of the lowest returns in 2022, making it difficult for them to recoup all their 2022 losses. Most pension providers in the OECD area suffered losses on their bond and equity investments in 2022, due to interest rate increases and falling equity valuations. Pension providers in some of the largest pension markets in Europe also experienced losses in other financial instruments or vehicles such as real estate (e.g. Netherlands) and interest-rate derivatives (e.g. Netherlands, the United Kingdom) in 2022 (OECD, 2023[12]). Positive returns in 2023 from rising equity valuations were insufficient to offset the losses in the largest pension markets.

By contrast, pension providers in other jurisdictions incurred lower losses in 2022, which they recouped more rapidly with a few exceptions. Likewise, public pension reserve funds that had a better investment performance in 2022 than other funds fared better over the two years. For example, Sweden's AP6 had a lower return than others in 2023 but made gains in 2022 and achieved profits over 2022-23, unlike most other AP funds.

Figure 2.5. Nominal investment rates of return, 2022-2023

In per cent

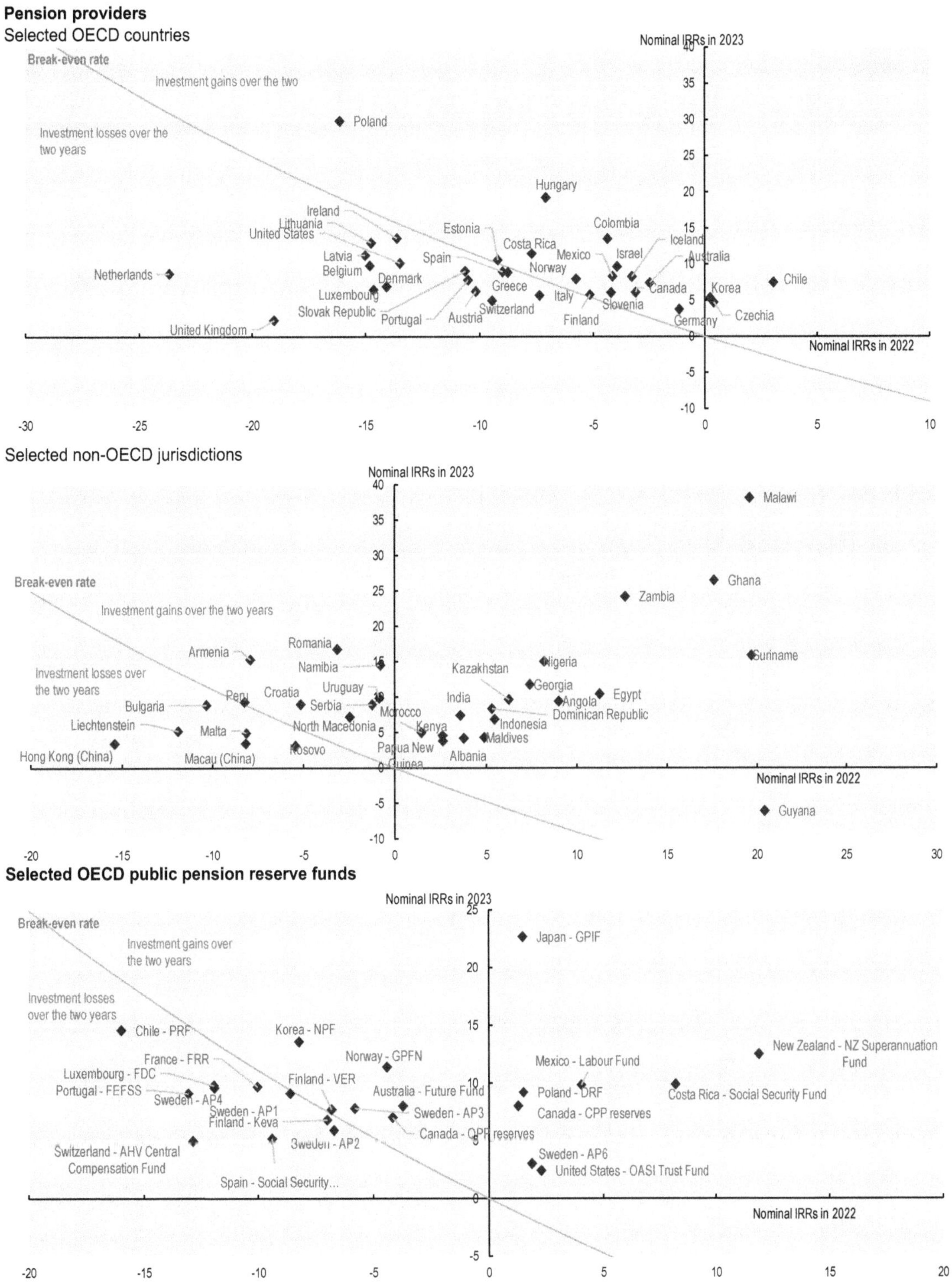

Note: For more details, please see the methodological notes in Annex C.

Source: OECD Global Pension Statistics and websites of public pension reserve funds.

StatLink https://stat.link/hbtpqg

2.3. The cashflow of contributions over expenditure supported asset growth in most jurisdictions except the United States and some European countries

The positive cashflow of contributions over benefit payments and other expenditure supported the growth of assets earmarked for retirement over 2022-23. Pension providers recorded a positive cashflow over the period in most jurisdictions (Figure 2.6), adding another source of revenue. Likewise, public pension reserve funds in Canada, Costa Rica and Korea benefitted from an excess of contributions over benefits to the PAYG public system which complemented investment gains (Figure 2.7).

Figure 2.6. Excess of contributions to pension providers over expenditure over 2022-23

As a % of assets at end-2021

Selected OECD countries

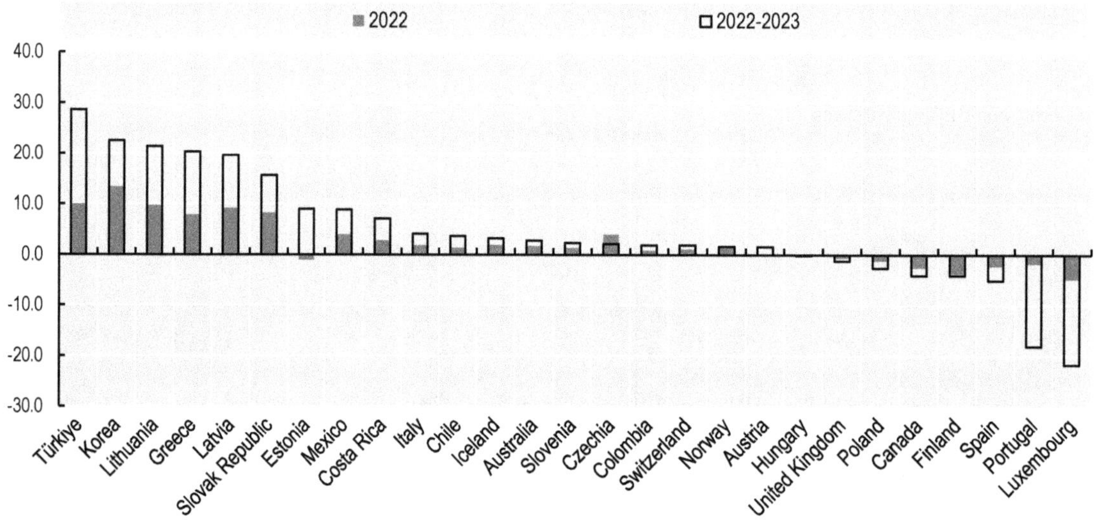

Selected other jurisdictions

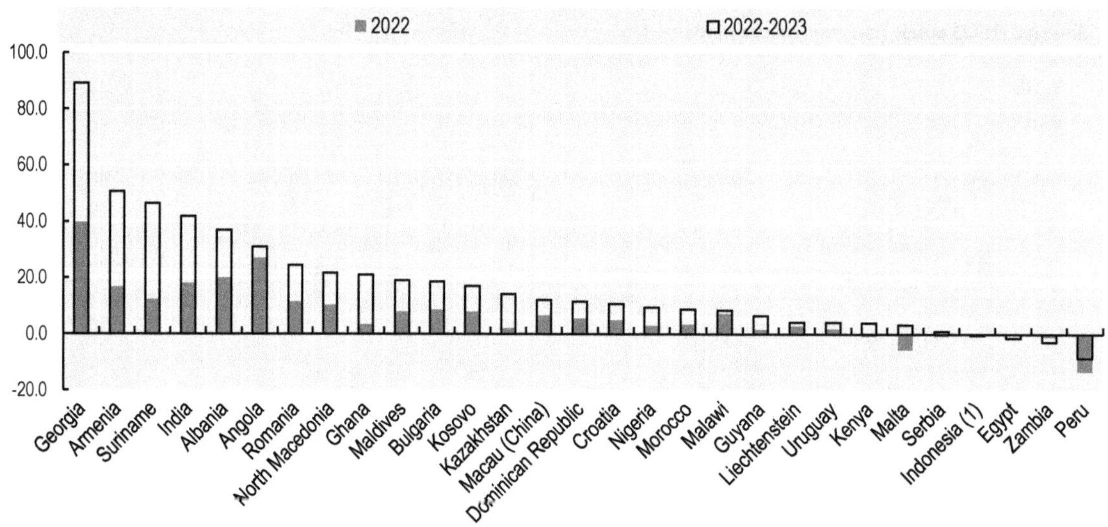

Note: For more details, please see the methodological notes in Annex C.
Source: OECD Global Pension Statistics.

StatLink https://stat.link/ifr9lg

Figure 2.7. Differences between inflows and outflows

As a % of assets at end-2021

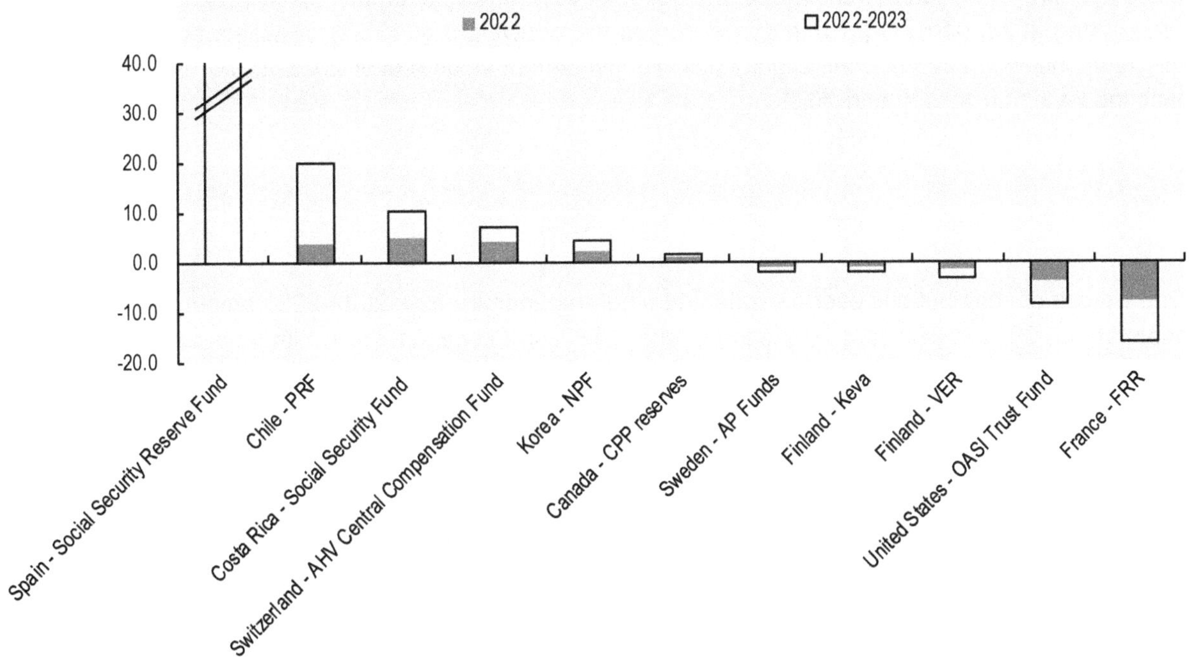

Source: OECD Global Pension Statistics and websites of public pension reserve funds.

StatLink https://stat.link/ou617d

The positive cashflows from contributions over benefits and other expenditure offset investment losses in several jurisdictions, especially in European countries that recently phased in asset-backed pensions (e.g. Bulgaria, Greece, Latvia, Lithuania, Slovak Republic). These countries benefitted from a large excess of contributions over benefits and other expenditure (over 15% of assets at end-2021), which exceeded investment losses.[1] The 2022 investment losses to offset were also relatively small in some of them (e.g. -8.7% in Greece, -8.1% in Malta) compared to more mature markets (-23.6% in the Netherlands, -19% in the United Kingdom). In the case of public pension reserve funds, the positive cashflows of the reserve funds of Chile, Spain and Switzerland offset the investment losses of these funds and brought the reserves to a higher level.

By contrast, the inflow of contributions was insufficient to offset investment losses in the United States and several European countries, in particular the largest European countries. The inflows of contributions exceeded benefits and expenditure in Austria and Liechtenstein but were not enough to take assets back to their 2021 level. Pension providers in some other European countries (Luxembourg, Spain, Portugal and the United Kingdom) even recorded a negative cashflow over 2022-23, which further reduced the amount of assets earmarked for retirement on top of the investment losses over 2022-23.

The negative cashflows that some mature countries experienced to finance benefits (e.g. Finland) reduced the amount of assets despite the positive investment income over the period 2022-23. For example, while pension providers in Finland managed to record a positive investment income in 2022 and 2023, assets declined due to higher payments and expenditure than contributions. Likewise, France (FRR), Finland, Sweden and the United States drew down their reserves to pay the benefits of the public PAYG systems, explaining the decline in assets of the public pension reserve funds despite the investment gains for some of them over the period 2022-23.

Early withdrawals as in the case of Peru offset the investment gains of pension providers over 2022-23. In Peru, members continued to benefit from the option of withdrawing their savings in 2022. In terms of cash flows, during 2022, pension providers in Peru lost the equivalent of 13.2% of assets at end-2021. The positive cashflow in 2023 and the slightly positive investment income over 2022-23 were not sufficient to reach the level of assets at end-2021.

Notes

[1] The excess of contributions over benefits and other expenditure over 2022-2023 amounted to 18.7% of assets at end-2021 in Bulgaria, 20.3% in Greece, 19.6% in Latvia, 21.4% in Lithuania and 15.6% in the Slovak Republic.

3 2023 marks a return to the long-term trend of growing assets earmarked for retirement

This section examines how the growth in assets in 2023 fits with longer term trends and analyses the drivers of these long-term trends.

Saving for retirement is for the long-term. It is therefore essential to look at developments in assets for retirement over a longer period than two years.

This section aims to examine how growth in assets in 2023 fits with longer term trends and analyse the drivers of these long-term trends.

This section first examines the growth in assets over the last two decades. It then looks at how the returns on investments of pension providers and public pension reserve funds have contributed to the long-term asset growth. It finally shows that the positive cashflow of contributions over expenditure also underpins the long-term growth in assets.

3.1. Assets more than tripled over the past two decades

Assets earmarked for retirement in the OECD area have more than tripled in USD current prices over the past two decades, despite fluctuations such as those seen in 2022-23. Pension systems have faced multiple events that led to losses in financial markets and a drop in total assets, such as the 2008 financial crisis or the COVID-19 outbreak in early 2020. Nevertheless, assets for retirement in the OECD area have consistently rebounded (Figure 3.1).

Figure 3.1. Assets earmarked for retirement in the OECD, 2001-2023

In USD trillion

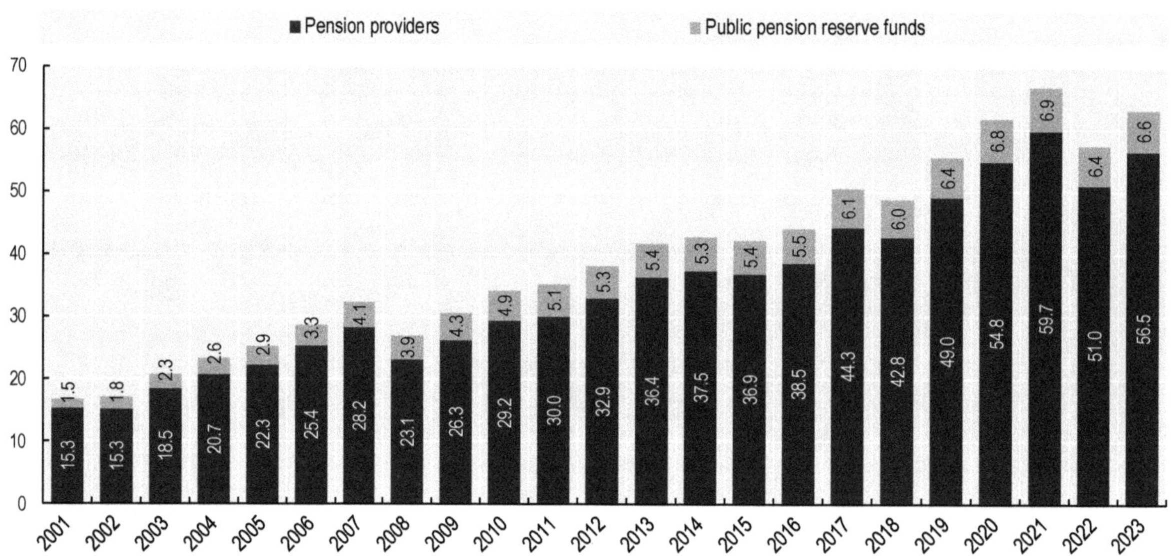

Note: For more details, please see the methodological notes in Annex C.
Source: OECD Global Pension Statistics and other sources.

StatLink https://stat.link/3qa87z

Assets have grown in all reporting jurisdictions over the last two decades, or since the beginning of the reporting period, despite several crises. Table 3.1 shows the average nominal growth rate of assets in 2023 and annually over the last 5, 10, 15 and 20 years up to end-2023. Over the last 15-20 years, the rise in assets has been the strongest among the countries that introduced their asset-backed pension system recently, such as Estonia, Latvia and Türkiye. However, it slowed down over the last five years in the first two, due to the investment losses in 2022, a maturing system with fewer new members joining (e.g. Latvia) or the recent option of withdrawing assets from the system (e.g. Estonia). Likewise, many non-OECD jurisdictions with recent systems recorded an average annual growth rate as strong or stronger than OECD countries (e.g. several other European and African countries). More mature systems had a lower long-term growth rate (e.g. United Kingdom and United States, between 5% and 6% per year on average over the last two decades).

Table 3.1. Geometric average annual nominal growth rate of assets of pension providers

In per cent

Selected OECD countries	Geometric average annual nominal growth rate				
	2023	5-yr	10-yr	15-yr	20-yr
Australia	8.8	5.8	7.6	7.4	9.5
Austria (1)	8.4	4.2	3.7	5.1	5.3
Canada	2.4	3.6	4.5	6.2	6.1
Chile	10.1	4.4	6.9	8.9	9.0
Colombia	15.8	11.1	12.0	12.4	16.1
Costa Rica (2)	16.9	13.6	15.6	16.9	17.9
Czechia	3.0	5.6	7.6	8.1	10.7
Denmark	0.2	4.6	4.5	5.1	6.3
Estonia	23.5	6.0	10.9	13.1	22.3
Finland	5.2	4.7	3.7	..	..
France (3)	6.0	5.1	4.8	6.0	..
Germany	6.1	2.6	4.5	5.5	6.3
Greece	22.4	10.0	8.6	32.2	..
Hungary (1)	21.3	6.5	6.7	-0.8	4.2
Iceland	10.5	11.5	10.6	10.4	11.8
Ireland	4.1	4.0	..	..	..
Israel	10.7	9.5	8.4	9.5	11.4
Italy	8.4	6.3	7.0	9.1	9.5
Japan	2.3	1.5	1.1	1.1	1.1
Korea	8.7	7.9	9.2	16.2	13.7
Latvia	23.8	14.1	15.2	16.8	27.0
Lithuania	27.0	17.8	16.5	..	..
Luxembourg	-14.7	-3.6	3.5	8.6	..
Mexico	12.4	11.4	9.9	11.2	..
Netherlands	8.6	3.2	5.0	5.8	6.1
New Zealand	10.4	11.1	13.0	13.9	11.4
Norway	8.4	6.4	6.7	7.8	7.9
Poland	34.9	9.2	-1.0	4.7	9.6
Portugal (4)	-8.8	1.0	3.5	0.3	1.1
Slovak Republic	17.3	11.0	9.4	12.1	..
Slovenia	7.3	6.3	6.2	7.5	14.7
Spain	4.4	1.5	1.2	1.7	2.9
Sweden	13.1	9.4	9.9	8.9	10.9
Switzerland	6.0	5.2	4.6	5.1	4.7
Türkiye (1)	73.3	51.7	40.2	37.3	..
United Kingdom	1.8	0.5	4.0	5.9	5.5
United States	12.1	7.0	5.5	7.1	5.9

Selected non-OECD jurisdictions	Geometric average annual nominal growth rate				
	2023	5-yr	10-yr	15-yr	20-yr
Albania	18.2	24.0	31.5	32.3	..
Angola	12.9	31.5	..	..	..
Armenia	42.2	38.1	..	..	..
Botswana	17.9	11.5	9.0	..	..
Brazil	15.5	9.5	..	..	..
Bulgaria	20.0	11.5	13.0	16.6	21.0
China	11.1	16.6	18.1	20.6	..
Croatia	15.6	9.3	10.7	13.5	18.9
Dominican Republic (2)	14.4	15.4	17.4	22.0	..
Egypt	10.0	14.4	14.7	13.1	..
Georgia	47.6	..	..	..	..
Ghana	47.2	31.3	..	..	..
Guyana	-2.2	11.7	10.4	11.0	..
Hong Kong (China)	2.2	4.2	6.0	7.7	9.6
Indonesia (5)	7.2	6.5	8.5	9.9	10.6
Jamaica	6.1	4.4	9.4	9.3	..
Kazakhstan	21.8	13.3	..	..	21.9
Kenya	9.3	8.1	9.5	13.1	13.7
Kosovo	12.1	9.9	11.4	..	..
Liechtenstein	7.1	7.5	7.1	9.2	..
Macau (China)	9.1	..	..	..	..
Malawi	48.1	28.8	30.0	..	..
Malaysia	19.2	19.2	35.9	..	..
Maldives	14.6	13.1	15.6	..	..
Malta	15.8	..	20.5	..	..
Morocco	10.3	5.6	..	..	..
Mozambique	18.0	13.5	..	..	..
Namibia	15.3	7.0	8.6	..	..
Nigeria	22.4	16.3	16.3	20.6	..
North Macedonia	18.7	16.1	17.7	24.7	..
Papua New Guinea	11.7	7.3	7.9	..	..
Peru	16.0	-4.7	1.9	6.2	9.0
Romania	31.4	21.5	24.5	39.1	..
Serbia	11.1	5.9	10.5	17.7	..
Singapore	4.3	7.6	8.3	..	..
Suriname	44.6	30.9	..	..	19.7
Uruguay	12.9	12.1	14.7	18.4	17.3
Zambia	25.8	15.2	14.3	15.4	14.5

Note: For more details, please see the methodological notes in Annex C.
Source: OECD Global Pension Statistics.

StatLink https://stat.link/ro9fz4

Trends in assets differ among public pension reserve funds. Some reserve funds have seen a decline over the long term, such as in France (FRR over the last 15 years), Spain (over the last 20 years) and the United States (over the last 10 years), with a depletion of their reserves (Table 3.2). Spain recently decided to reverse course and to replenish its reserve fund, which explains the positive average growth rate over the more recent period.

Table 3.2. Geometric average annual nominal growth rate of assets of public pension reserve funds

In per cent

	Geometric average annual nominal growth rate				
	2023	5-yr	10-yr	15-yr	20-yr
Australia - Future Fund	8.0	7.6	8.2	8.8	..
Canada - CPP reserves	10.3	9.7	11.2	11.8	11.4
Canada - QPP reserves	13.6	10.7	10.2	10.9	9.9
Chile - PRF	34.3	2.3	7.0	11.0	..
Costa Rica - Social Security Fund	9.9	6.9	..	..	..
Finland - Keva	5.6	5.4	5.6	..	..
Finland - VER	5.9	4.3	..	..	..
France - AGIRC-ARRCO	15.9	5.7	..	..	..
France - FRR	-0.5	-8.3	-5.2	-1.8	1.3
Israel - NIF	0.2	1.8	2.9	5.1	..
Japan - GPIF	18.2	8.4	5.8	4.5	6.0
Korea - NPF	16.3	10.1	9.3	..	11.5
Luxembourg - FDC	11.7	7.7	7.2	8.9	..
Mexico - Labour Fund	13.6	..	..	..	..
New Zealand - NZ Superannuation Fund	19.6	13.2	10.7	12.4	17.1
Norway - GPFN	11.4	8.2	7.7	9.7	..
Poland - DRF	12.9	8.6	13.8	19.4	27.7
Portugal - FEFSS	29.7	11.4	9.8	8.9	8.9
Spain - Social Security Reserve Fund	160.6	2.0	-20.3	-14.4	-3.8
Sweden - AP Funds	6.8	7.1	6.3	7.0	6.3
Switzerland - AHV Central Compensation Fund	6.1	2.8	1.5	1.8	3.5
United States - OASI Trust Fund	-2.6	-1.1	-0.1	1.2	3.4

Source: OECD Global Pension Statistics and websites of public pension reserve funds.

StatLink https://stat.link/utpmvd

3.2. Investment income has contributed to this long-term growth in assets

Pension providers and public pension reserve funds have achieved investment gains over the long-term, contributing to the nominal growth of assets earmarked for retirement. Pension providers have managed to record positive average nominal rates of return over the last 10, 15 and 20 years in all reporting jurisdictions (Table 3.3). Average nominal rates of return are also positive over the last five years, despite large investment losses in 2022 in some countries (e.g. Netherlands). Türkiye has the highest average nominal rates of return over the last 5, 10 and 15 years, driven by large price increases in the financial instruments pension providers hold. Likewise, most public pension reserve funds have earned a positive investment income over the last two decades, which has a been a source of financing of reserves for the public PAYG arrangements.

Table 3.3. Average annual investment rates of return

In per cent

	Nominal average annual IRR over the last				Real average annual IRR over the last			
	5 years	10 years	15 years	20 years	5 years	10 years	15 years	20 years
	Panel A. Pension providers: selected OECD countries							
Australia	5.7	7.3	6.3	6.9	2.2	4.5	3.7	4.1
Austria	3.1	2.9	3.6	3.1	-1.3	-0.1	0.8	0.5
Belgium	3.7	4.0	5.2	4.9	0.0	1.4	2.7	2.4
Canada	5.6	6.1	6.9	6.4	2.0	3.4	4.5	4.1
Chile	6.9	6.7	7.3	6.8	1.0	2.0	3.5	2.7
Colombia	8.3	7.8	9.0	9.8	1.6	2.0	4.2	4.6
Costa Rica	8.1	7.9	8.4	..	5.7	5.6	5.3	..
Czechia	1.7	1.3	1.5	2.0	-4.8	-2.7	-1.7	-1.2
Denmark	3.4	4.2	5.1	5.2	0.7	2.5	3.3	3.3
Estonia	4.9	3.5	4.4	3.2	-1.8	-0.5	0.8	-1.0
Finland	6.1	5.3	..	..	2.6	3.2	..	..
Germany	2.9	3.2	3.6	3.7	-0.6	0.9	1.6	1.7
Greece	3.4	3.6	..	..	0.6	2.4	..	..
Hungary	5.2	5.1	..	..	-3.1	0.2	..	..
Iceland	9.1	7.7	7.8	8.0	3.3	3.8	3.6	2.8
Ireland	7.8	..	..	..	4.0	..	..	..
Israel	7.2	5.6	7.1	..	4.9	4.5	5.5	..
Italy	2.2	2.2	2.8	2.9	-1.0	0.3	1.0	1.0
Latvia	2.7	2.1	3.3	2.8	-3.0	-1.5	0.4	-1.5
Lithuania	5.7	4.4	..	..	-1.2	0.2	..	..
Luxembourg	1.4	1.9	2.9	..	-1.6	-0.1	0.8	..
Mexico	7.3	5.7	6.7	..	2.0	1.0	2.2	..
Netherlands	2.1	4.1	5.8	5.0	-1.9	1.5	3.3	2.8
Norway	5.3	5.1	5.9	5.7	1.5	1.9	3.2	3.1
Poland	6.2	..	..	..	-1.1	..	..	..
Portugal	2.4	2.6	3.0	3.4	-0.3	0.9	1.4	1.6
Slovak Republic	2.5	2.1	2.0	..	-3.5	-1.2	-0.9	..
Slovenia	2.6	3.8	4.3	..	-1.3	1.5	2.1	..
Spain	3.3	2.7	3.3	..	0.2	0.9	1.5	..
Switzerland	3.3	3.2	3.9	3.3	2.2	2.7	3.5	2.7
Türkiye	31.0	20.1	16.4	..	-4.0	-2.6	-1.2	..
United States	5.3	3.8	5.0	3.2	1.2	1.0	2.4	0.6
	Panel B. Pension providers: selected non-OECD jurisdictions							
Albania	3.7	4.2	5.1	..	0.3	1.6	2.4	..
Angola	7.4	..	..	..	-10.9	..	..	..
Armenia	6.6	7.2	..	..	2.6	4.4	..	..
Bulgaria	2.3	2.7	3.4	3.3	-3.9	-0.9	0.3	-0.8
Croatia	3.8	5.0	..	..	-0.8	2.5	..	..
Dominican Republic	9.0	9.6	10.7	..	3.0	5.4	6.1	..
Egypt	12.2	..	..	..	-1.7	..	..	..
Georgia	9.4	..	..	..	2.6	..	..	..
Guyana	9.7	..	..	..	5.9	..	..	..
Hong Kong (China)	1.8	1.8	3.8	..	0.1	-0.3	1.1	..
India	7.8	..	..	..	1.9	..	..	..
Indonesia (1)	7.0	8.3	..	..	4.1	4.5	..	..
Kazakhstan	8.5	..	..	..	-1.5	..	..	..
Kosovo	3.7	3.2	..	..	-0.6	0.6	..	..

	Nominal average annual IRR over the last				Real average annual IRR over the last			
	5 years	10 years	15 years	20 years	5 years	10 years	15 years	20 years
Liechtenstein	2.4	2.3	3.0	..	1.3	1.8	2.7	..
Macau (China)	1.4	..	..	..	0.4	..	..	..
Malawi	20.2	20.1	..	..	2.1	2.4	..	..
Maldives	4.9	5.8	..	..	3.8	4.8	..	..
Nigeria	11.7	11.2	..	..	-5.8	-3.7	..	..
North Macedonia	5.7	5.3	6.1	..	-0.1	2.1	3.2	..
Peru	5.0	4.9	6.3	6.2	0.4	1.1	2.8	2.8
Romania	7.4	6.0	..	..	0.1	1.7	..	..
Serbia	4.0	6.6	7.7	..	-2.5	2.2	2.2	..
Suriname	17.1	..	..	..	-16.8	..	..	..
Uruguay	8.7	10.4	14.2	..	0.7	2.2	5.9	..
Zambia	15.2	14.8	14.4	..	1.0	2.6	3.6	..
	Panel C. Selected public pension reserve funds							
Australia - Future Fund	7.6	8.1	8.8	..	3.8	5.3	6.0	..
Canada - CPP reserves	7.7	9.2	10.1	8.2	4.2	6.5	7.6	5.9
Canada - QPP reserves	7.0	8.0	8.8	7.4	3.4	5.3	6.4	5.1
Chile - PRF	8.3	8.0	4.9	..	2.2	3.2	1.2	..
Finland - Keva	6.3	5.7	7.0	..	2.8	3.6	5.0	..
Finland - VER	6.4	5.4	6.4	5.5	2.8	3.3	4.4	3.5
France - FRR	3.2	3.4	4.6	3.5	0.4	1.6	2.9	1.8
Japan - GPIF	9.3	6.8	6.4	5.0	7.7	5.6	5.6	4.4
Korea - NPF	7.1	5.6	6.0	5.8	4.4	3.6	3.8	3.4
Luxembourg - FDC	5.3	4.8	4.8	..	2.2	2.7	2.6	..
New Zealand - NZ Superannuation Fund	9.1	10.1	12.4	9.9	4.9	7.4	9.8	7.2
Norway - GPFN	8.2	7.8	9.8	7.8	4.3	4.5	7.0	5.1
Poland - DRF	2.4	2.6	3.7	4.6	-4.6	-1.2	0.2	1.2
Spain - Social Security Reserve Fund	-1.1	0.7	1.9	2.5	-4.1	-1.1	0.1	0.3
Sweden - AP1	8.7	8.0	8.7	..	4.1	5.1	6.3	..
Sweden - AP2	6.6	6.8	8.1	6.9	2.0	3.9	5.8	4.8
Sweden - AP3	9.6	8.7	8.9	7.6	4.9	5.8	6.6	5.5
Sweden - AP4	9.0	8.6	9.6	7.9	4.3	5.6	7.2	5.8
Sweden - AP6	15.3	12.3	10.2	8.9	10.4	9.3	7.9	6.8
Switzerland - AHV Central Compensation Fund	1.8	2.8	..	..	0.7	2.2	..	..
United States - OASI Trust Fund	2.5	2.8	3.3	3.8	-1.5	0.1	0.8	1.2

Note: For more details, please see the methodological notes in Annex C.
Source: OECD Global Pension Statistics and websites of public pension reserve funds.

StatLink https://stat.link/cumpeb

Pension providers in Latin America recorded the largest average rates of return in real terms over the long-term. Pension providers in Colombia had an average annual real rate of return of 4.6% over the last 20 years, the highest among those with available data. Pension providers in Costa Rica, the Dominican Republic and Uruguay had among the highest real rates of return over the last 15 years, above 5%. Real investment returns tended to be lower during more recent periods in Latin American countries. Mesa-Lago (2021[13]) argues that the decline in investment returns may be partly due to a reduction in interest rates, given that bonds account for a significant percentage of investments of pension providers.[1]

By contrast, the lowest average real rates of return were recorded mostly in Europe and Türkiye where pension providers had a conservative asset allocation or were facing high inflation. Pension providers recorded investment losses in real terms in Czechia, the Slovak Republic and Türkiye over the last 15 years, and in Bulgaria, Czechia, Estonia and Latvia over the last 20 years. The relatively conservative asset allocation in these countries may have contributed to these losses in real terms in the long run, as pension providers earned lower returns than others when stock markets were performing strongly.[2] The large losses that pension providers incurred in 2022, also on bond holdings, further exacerbated these losses over the long-term.[3] Inflation has also been higher in some of these countries (e.g. Estonia, Türkiye) than in others for some years, requiring higher returns in nominal terms to catch up with inflation.[4]

Likewise, public pension reserve funds that invested mostly in bonds have earned a lower investment income over the long term than others with a more diversified portfolio. Reserve funds with more diversified portfolios achieved the largest investment gains. Public pension reserve funds recorded a real investment rate of return above 5% per year on average over the last 20 years in Canada, Norway, Sweden (AP3, AP4 and AP6) and New Zealand. Japan's GPIF recorded an average annual real investment rate of return close to 5% over the last 20 years and above 5% in the last 15 years. These funds have had a more diversified portfolio than others, such as the public pension reserve funds in Spain and the United States that hold only government bonds and had an average return just slightly above inflation over the last 20 years.

Pension providers had been looking for higher yielding instruments than bonds when interest rates were falling in the last decades. Figure 3.2 shows the average asset allocation of pension providers in 15 jurisdictions over 2001-23. Figure 3.2 shows that the proportion of assets invested in bonds has been falling over the last two decades, with a temporary spike in 2008 as a result of a sharp fall in equity valuations. By contrast, pension providers have increased their exposure to equities and in alternative investments. Pension providers in Latin America have started investing in alternative assets over the last decades.[5] In the United Kingdom, the low interest rate environment and low returns have led larger pension schemes to look at alternative investments such as hedge funds and private equity (PPI, 2024[14]). Some have been increasing their exposure to foreign assets (e.g. Chile, Peru and some European countries with small capital markets) in search of potentially higher risk-adjusted returns. Public pension reserve funds in Korea and Japan have also sought to further diversify their asset allocation to achieve higher returns (OECD, 2022[15]; OECD, 2021[9]).

Figure 3.2. Average asset allocation of pension providers in selected asset classes and investment vehicles in a selection of 15 jurisdictions, 2001-2023

As a percentage of total investment

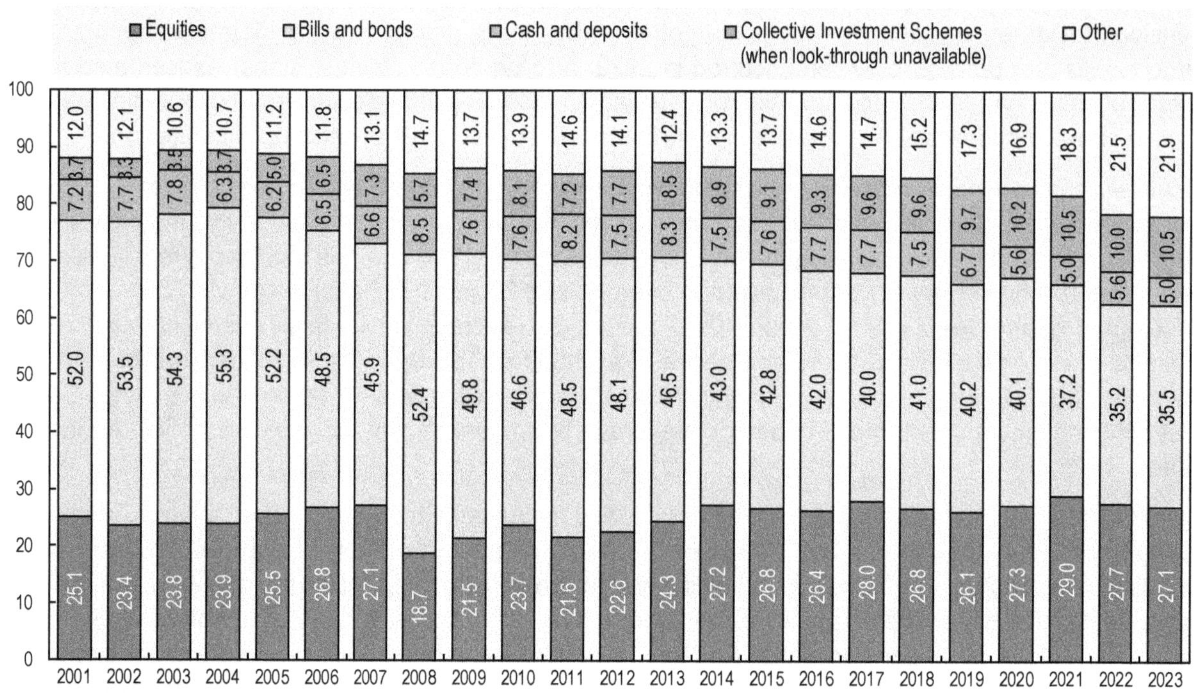

Note: For more details, please see the methodological notes in Annex C.
Source: OECD Global Pension Statistics.

StatLink https://stat.link/f2kjcp

Policy makers have encouraged the diversification of the asset allocation of pension providers by loosening investment regulations. For example, Estonia and Latvia raised the investment limit in equities from 75% to 100% in 2019 and 2021 respectively (OECD, 2024[16]), which may have contributed to the rise in the proportion of assets invested in equities by pension providers in these two countries.[6] Peru has also progressively lifted investment regulations on foreign investments to allow pension providers to seek investment gains abroad. Some countries have also encouraged investing in alternative investments by removing barriers for investments and allowing these investments or increasing the limits (e.g. in Czechia, Colombia, Switzerland). For example, Czechia passed a law in 2023 allowing pension management companies to establish alternative funds that can invest in alternative assets such as private equity funds, real estate and start-ups.

The change in default investment strategies may also have played a role in the reduction in bond holdings in the investment portfolio of pension providers. Members of defined contribution pension plans can usually decide the ways in which their assets are invested. Default investment strategies are for those unwilling or unable to make a choice. Policy makers have favoured less conservative investment strategies by making people default into investment allocations with more growth assets (e.g. Croatia in 2019 and New Zealand in 2021),[7] or moving away from a fixed asset allocation towards life cycle asset allocation, for example. Lithuania, the Slovak Republic and Slovenia, for example, have established life-cycle funds where members' assets are more exposed to higher-risk higher-return assets in their youth (e.g. in 2019 in Lithuania, in 2023 in the Slovak Republic and in 2016 in Slovenia for voluntary pension insurance). The share invested in equities has grown in Croatia, Lithuania and New Zealand.[8] The share in bonds has declined in the Slovak Republic and Slovenia, but the proportion of assets in equities remains relatively small.[9]

The rise in interest rates had led to a renewed focus in government bonds in several countries, such as in Bulgaria and Colombia, reversing the decline in bond holdings (since 2019 in Bulgaria, 2018 in Colombia).[10] The largest reallocation towards bonds occurred in Colombia between 2022 and 2023 (by 12 percentage points). Pension providers in Colombia increased their exposure to fixed-income securities linked to inflation, as this asset class was generating more alpha.

3.3. A positive cashflow of contributions over expenditure also underpinned the long-term growth of assets

A positive cashflow of contributions over benefits and other expenditure also underpinned the growth of assets earmarked for retirement in recent years. Contributions exceeded benefits and other expenditure, with a positive average annual cash flow in most jurisdictions over the last 5 to 20 years (Table 3.4).

Table 3.4. Average annual excess of contributions over benefits and other expenditure over the long-term

As % of assets at end-2023

Selected OECD countries	2023	last 5 years	last 10 years	last 15 years	last 20 years
Australia	1.0	0.2	0.2	0.4	0.6
Austria	1.7	0.7	0.5	..	..
Canada	-1.5	-2.1	-1.1	-0.5	-0.4
Chile	2.0	-2.5	-0.4	0.2	0.3
Colombia	1.0	1.5	1.8	1.4	1.3
Costa Rica	3.8	3.2	3.2	2.6	..
Czechia	-1.7	3.2	4.1	3.6	3.4
Estonia	9.0	-0.8	3.4	3.2	3.2
Finland	-0.4	-1.1	..	..	..
Greece	10.2	4.9	..	..	..
Hungary	0.0	0.7	0.9	-7.1	-2.1
Iceland	1.2	1.2	1.3	1.0	1.0
Italy	2.2	2.8	2.9	2.9	2.6
Latvia	9.0	7.5	6.3	4.8	4.1
Lithuania	9.7	7.0	5.3	..	..
Luxembourg	-24.3	-6.0	0.6	2.3	..
Mexico	4.3	3.3	2.9	2.4	..
Norway	0.1	0.6	0.8	0.8	0.8
Poland	-1.3	-1.3	-8.3	-2.1	0.2
Portugal	-20.9	-3.4	-0.7	-3.5	-2.7
Slovak Republic	6.4	6.1	4.5	4.3	..
Slovenia	0.9	2.9	1.8	1.8	..
Spain	-3.1	-1.2	-0.8	-1.2	..
Switzerland	0.9	1.4	1.0	0.7	0.8
Türkiye	6.0	3.2	..	..	..

Selected non-OECD jurisdictions	2023	last 5 years	last 10 years	last 15 years	last 20 years
Albania	11.5	10.8	7.8	5.4	..
Armenia	20.5	12.5	..	..	..
Bulgaria	8.6	6.5	5.5	4.7	3.9
Croatia	5.2	4.0	3.4	..	..
Dominican Republic	4.8	3.8	..	..	..
Egypt	-0.8	0.9	..	..	..
Guyana	3.9	0.8	..	..	..
India	15.2	10.4	..	..	..
Indonesia (1)	0.0	-0.6	-0.2	..	..
Kazakhstan	9.2	3.0	..	..	..
Kosovo	7.9	4.7	4.6	..	..
Liechtenstein	1.5	3.9	3.2	3.1	..
Malawi	0.6	2.0	1.5	..	..
Maldives	8.8	5.9	..	..	..
Nigeria	4.7	2.3	1.9	..	..
North Macedonia	9.1	6.6	5.4	4.4	..
Peru	5.1	-12.3	-4.2	-1.9	-0.8
Romania	9.2	7.4	5.9	..	..
Serbia	1.5	1.4	2.0	2.5	..
Suriname	17.5	6.1	..	..	..
Uruguay	2.1	2.0	..	..	..

Selected OECD countries	2023	last 5 years	last 10 years	last 15 years	last 20 years
United Kingdom	-0.9	-1.3	..	..	..

Selected non-OECD jurisdictions	2023	last 5 years	last 10 years	last 15 years	last 20 years

Note: For more details, please see the methodological notes in Annex C.
Source: OECD Global Pension Statistics.

StatLink https://stat.link/9ersa7

Growing pension contributions are one of the factors behind the positive cashflow of pension providers over the years. Most reporting jurisdictions recorded a nominal growth of contributions paid over the last 5, 10, 15 and 20 years (Table 3.5).[11] Albania, Latvia, North Macedonia and Romania experienced some of the largest excesses of contributions over benefits and other expenditure and also had some of the largest growth rates of contributions over the last 10 years or more. The few exceptions where contributions declined include countries that transferred the assets of some asset-backed pension arrangements to the public pension system, such as Hungary (in 2011), Poland (in 2014) and Portugal (for a pension fund in 2023). These countries therefore tend to have negative cashflows over periods covering these reforms, with a reduction in contributions and an increase in expenditure from transfers. Contributions started growing again following the change in the system such as in Hungary and Poland, with a positive nominal growth in assets over the last 10 years.

Table 3.5. Geometric average nominal growth rate of contributions paid to pension providers

In per cent

Selected OECD countries	2023	last 5 years	last 10 years	last 15 years	last 20 years
Australia	13.4	7.8	4.9	2.9	6.2
Canada	0.7	1.9	2.5	3.6	4.1
Chile	5.8	10.3	9.2	9.9	10.5
Costa Rica	14.0	7.5	7.9	..	..
Czechia	0.4	3.2	3.1	..	..
Denmark	8.0	5.9	5.8	5.0	5.3
Estonia	7.8	1.5	5.7	4.6	11.7
Finland	2.4	3.8	3.1	..	..
Germany	-6.6	-10.5	3.4	2.3	5.6
Hungary	9.3	2.7	4.5	-6.6	-2.8
Iceland	10.8	9.1	12.9	8.8	..
Italy	5.4	3.3	4.4	3.9	..
Korea	-6.5	9.4	11.5	25.6	27.2
Latvia	15.2	9.2	13.3	..	..
Lithuania	17.6	14.1	18.4	..	..
Luxembourg	-5.7	-7.3	3.1	5.5	..
Mexico	22.7	12.8	10.3	7.6	..
Netherlands	-9.7	4.7	1.8	2.8	3.5
New Zealand	9.9	10.0	12.3	..	..
Norway	21.3	12.2	6.9	3.7	6.3
Poland	21.9	23.1	4.0	-0.8	3.1
Portugal	-20.6	-13.7	..	..	..

Selected non-OECD jurisdictions	2023	last 5 years	last 10 years	last 15 years	last 20 years
Albania	-3.4	15.0	11.1	21.6	..
Angola	-66.1	18.7	..	..	..
Armenia	21.6	25.2	..	..	..
Bulgaria	13.8	10.5	10.5	8.6	14.0
Croatia	4.3	7.7	..	..	..
Guyana	4.3	8.4	..	..	..
Hong Kong (China)	2.7	2.3	4.0	5.1	5.1
Kazakhstan	25.2	20.6	..	..	..
Liechtenstein	8.0	4.2	4.0	6.3	..
Malawi	21.9	15.1	..	..	..
Maldives	10.8	8.7	8.4	..	..
Malta	24.4	..	-4.0	..	..
North Macedonia	20.0	13.4	12.7	12.7	..
Peru	2.3	3.1	6.8	7.8	10.4
Romania	16.8	10.9	15.1	19.8	..
Serbia	18.6	5.0	5.1	..	..
Suriname	23.9	..	..	..	15.7
Uruguay	12.0	10.5	..	..	..
Zambia	3.2	16.6	11.7	12.4	10.0

Selected OECD countries	2023	last 5 years	last 10 years	last 15 years	last 20 years
Slovak Republic	12.0	13.2	11.4	-4.1	..
Slovenia	4.2	5.4	4.7	1.8	..
Spain	9.0	-9.3	-4.4	-6.2	-3.9
Switzerland	3.3	3.2	2.0	2.3	3.7
Türkiye	112.0	41.9	31.8	22.8	..
United Kingdom	-1.3	..	2.6	3.9	4.3

Selected non-OECD jurisdictions	2023	last 5 years	last 10 years	last 15 years	last 20 years

Source: OECD Global Pension Statistics.

StatLink https://stat.link/gibrhj

Increases in contributions have several explanations. These include an increase in the proportion of people participating in a pension plan, developments in labour markets and changes in contribution rates.

In some countries, the growth in contributions comes from an increase in the proportion of people participating in a pension plan. Countries with the largest increases in contributions are those where the proportion of people participating in a pension plan has increased significantly, such as in Armenia, Bulgaria, Estonia, Latvia and New Zealand (Figure 3.3). The common feature of all these countries is that they introduced mandatory pension arrangements or automatic enrolment programmes.

Figure 3.3. Evolution of the proportion of the working-age population participating in a pension plan, by type of plan, over the longest available period for each jurisdiction

As a % of the working-age population

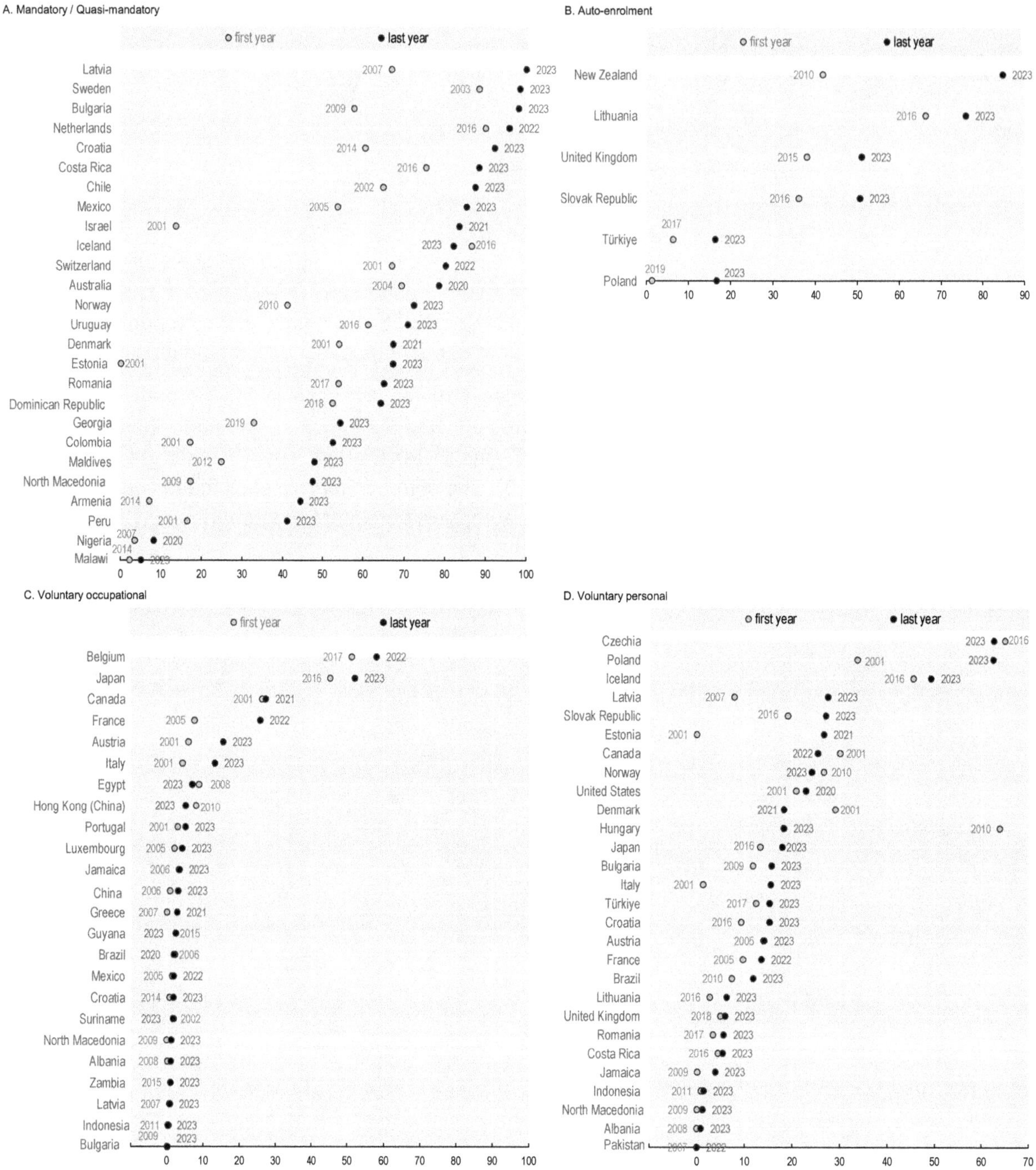

Note: For more details, please see the methodological notes in Annex C.
Source: OECD Global Pension Statistics and other sources.

StatLink https://stat.link/npek47

Participation has increased in most types of pension plans. This growth was more moderate in voluntary arrangements. Countries have tried to encourage participation in a pension plan by introducing mandatory plans (e.g. Greece) or automatic enrolment programmes (e.g. New Zealand, Poland, Türkiye, the United Kingdom), expanding the base of people eligible for a plan (e.g. Australia, Norway), facilitating the set-up of plans by employers (e.g. Spain), reducing the burden for employers to set up a plan (e.g. in the United States) and designing plans targeting a specific population (e.g. informal workers in several African countries). Countries have also used financial incentives and communication campaigns to encourage people to contribute.

Developments in labour markets and wage growth also influence participation and contributions to pension plans. A higher proportion of people working improves the access of the working-age population to workplace pension arrangements. Contributions also rise mechanically when they are a fixed percentage of the salary and salaries increase. Improvement in employment rates after COVID-19 is likely to have contributed to the increase in the number of people participating in a pension plan and in contributions. The rise in nominal wages, recently driven to some extent by inflation, also contributed to the rise in contributions in nominal terms. Rises in inflation led to faster growth in contributions over the last 5 years than over the last 10, 15 and 20 years, such as in Türkiye.

Several countries increased contribution rates, leading to a rise in contributions. For example, Australia has been increasing the mandatory contribution rate for employers by 0.5 percentage point every year since 2021 (to reach 12% in 2025),[12] which may explain the acceleration of the growth in pension contributions in recent years. In New Zealand, the minimum contribution rates to KiwiSaver plans rose from 2% to 3% of gross salary for both employees and employers in 2013. The United Kingdom increased the minimum contribution rates in occupational plans with automatic enrolment from 1% to 2% of qualifying earnings for employers and from 1% to 3% for employees in 2018, and then to 3% for employers and 5% for employees in 2019. Mexico also decided in 2020 to increase mandatory employer contributions and adjusted government contributions starting from 2023. Türkiye recently raised the state matching contributions from 25% to 30% for people joining the individual pension system.

Benefits have also increased in many jurisdictions but the cashflows of contributions over benefit payments remain positive over the long-term except in a few cases. Negative cashflows in Table 3.4 may have different causes: the maturity of the system with benefit payments exceeding contributions for years (e.g. Canada, Finland, United Kingdom), early withdrawals during COVID-19 (e.g. Chile, Peru), change in the rules on contributions (e.g. Estonia)[13] and transfer of assets to the public PAYG system (e.g. Hungary, Poland, Portugal).

Notes

[1] See Annex B

[2] In Estonia, the proportion invested in equities only rose recently, which may be due to the lifting of investment regulations on equity investments in 2019. The proportion in equities also increased over the years in Latvia, from 19% of assets at end-2015 to 51% at end-2023.

[3] The real investment rate of return of pension providers was -23.3% in Bulgaria in 2022, -13.3 in Czechia, -22.8% in Estonia, -29.7% in Latvia, -22.5% in the Slovak Republic.

[4] The return of Estonian pension funds is on its way to number one in the Baltics | SEB

[5] See Preqin | Alternative Assets Data, Solutions and Insights and What Latin American pension funds are looking for (privateequityinternational.com)

[6] See Annex B.

[7] New KiwiSaver default providers – Information for KiwiSaver members

[8] The proportion of assets invested in equities grew from 23% at end-2014 to 28% at end-2023 in Croatia, from 39% at end-2010 to 70% at end-2023 in Lithuania, from 27% at end-2014 to 43% at end-2023 in New Zealand. See Annex B for the full series.

[9] The proportion of assets in bonds increased up to 2014 before declining afterwards in the Slovak Republic. The proportion of assets invested in bonds declined from 75% at end-2003 to 56% at end-2023 for all pension providers combined in Slovenia. In both countries, the proportion of assets in equities remained below 10% in nearly all years. See Annex B

[10] See Annex B

[11] See Annex B for the time series of contributions paid to pension providers as % of GDP.

[12] Super guarantee | Australian Taxation Office (ato.gov.au)

[13] The pension reform in 2021 in Estonia allowed members to apply for an exemption from making contributions to the second pillar. See Pensions in Estonia | EURAXESS

4 The long-term shift away from defined benefit plans continued

This section examines whether the funding ratio of defined benefit plans continued to improve in 2023 and whether this has had implications on the long-term shift away from these plans.

While assets have been growing over the long-term, liabilities of defined benefit (DB) plans have been growing too and faster than assets in some countries, putting pressure on the sponsors of these plans. The deterioration of the funding ratio – i.e. the ratio of assets over liabilities – has led some employers to shift away from these plans towards defined contribution (DC) plans. However, the funding ratio of DB plans improved in a number of countries in 2022 following the rise in interest rates.

This section looks at whether the funding ratio of DB plans continued to improve in 2023 and whether this had had implications on the long-term shift away from DB plans.[1] This section shows that the liabilities of DB plans also grew in 2023. However, assets grew at a faster pace than liabilities, leading to an improvement in the funding ratio. Despite this, the shift from DB to DC continued.

4.1. Liabilities of defined benefit plans grew again in 2023 after a decline in 2022

After a decline in 2022 in most jurisdictions, the liabilities of DB plans grew again in 2023. Liabilities have been increasing over the last decades, driven by years of falling interest rates and improving life expectancy.[2] The increase in interest rates in 2022 temporarily reversed this trend for pension providers using market-based discount rates (e.g. Netherlands, United Kingdom). For these providers, higher interest rates translated into higher discount rates to calculate the present value of the liabilities, leading to a decline in the liabilities of pension providers. Yet, liabilities rose again for pension providers in all reporting jurisdictions in 2023 except in Ireland, Luxembourg and the United Kingdom (Figure 4.1).[3] The discount rates that the largest private pension funds used in the United States fluctuated in 2023 but ended up at a lower level at end-2023 than at end-2022 (Milliman, 2024[17]). As a result, the liabilities of these funds were higher at end-2023 than the year before. Liabilities increased in Finland and Iceland where pension providers value liabilities using a fixed discount rate (at 3% and 3.5% respectively). The liabilities shown in Figure 4.1 are aggregated at the national level and reflect the evolution of funds. The evolution of the liabilities may therefore reflect the population of DB plans.

Figure 4.1. Evolution of the liabilities of defined benefit plans in selected jurisdictions, 2001-2023

Base: 2021 = 100

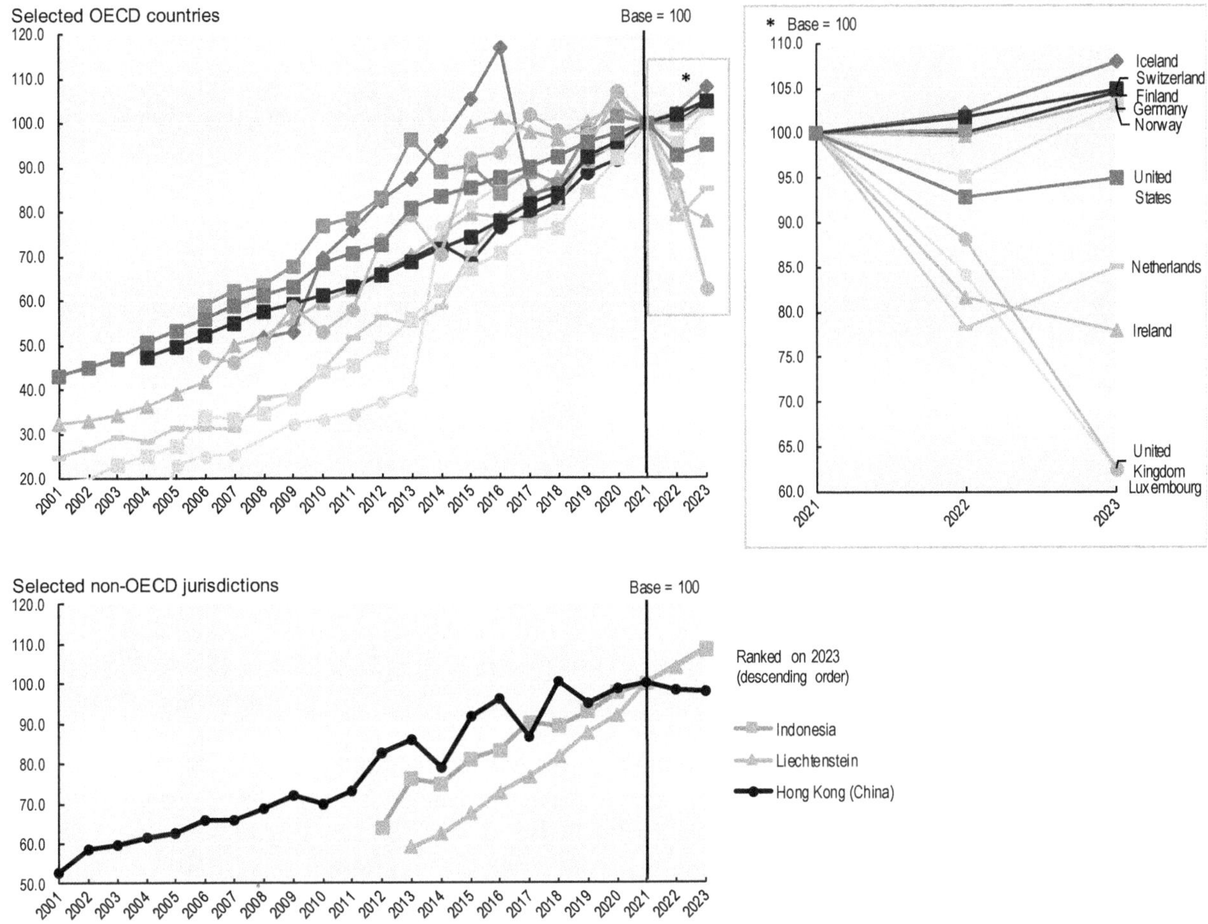

Note: For more details, please see the methodological notes in Annex C.
Source: OECD Global Pension Statistics.

StatLink https://stat.link/g2rywa

4.2. Assets outpaced liabilities in 2023

Assets outpaced liabilities in 2023, leading to an improvement in the funding ratio, which is the ratio of assets over liabilities. The funding ratio of DB plans improved in 2023 in Finland, Germany, Ireland, Liechtenstein, Norway, Switzerland, the United Kingdom and the United States. It reached a record high in the United Kingdom and the United States, although the funding ratio remained below 100% in the United States. A ratio below 100% means that the assets would be insufficient to meet all the liabilities of a plan (Table 4.1).

Table 4.1. Funding ratio of defined benefit plans in selected jurisdictions

In per cent

	2003	2008	2013	2018	2019	2020	2021	2022	2023
Selected OECD countries									
Finland	..	..	125.3	124.6	124.7	129.4	137.2	125.3	126.6
Germany	105.2	105.4	112.2	122.9	129.9	132.9	132.0	116.0	118.2
Iceland	..	39.7	58.7	32.0	32.0	32.5	32.6	27.6	25.9
Ireland	..	..	..	106.0	110.7	111.0	122.2	128.5	131.2
Luxembourg	..	..	100.2	100.9	101.0	101.3	101.1	104.4	100.2
Mexico	..	84.3	75.3	66.9	62.0	60.2	66.7	65.7	..
Netherlands	103.0	110.3	111.2	104.2	105.0	101.3	115.4	116.1	116.0
Norway	112.1	110.9	111.5	114.5	114.5	114.8	114.6	115.4	115.5
Switzerland	..	94.8	106.0	105.2	110.0	112.3	117.3	106.0	109.1
United Kingdom	..	99.4	84.1	95.7	99.2	94.9	102.8	113.1	134.3
United States	66.0	52.4	57.0	56.6	61.3	65.4	69.4	67.9	72.0
Selected non-OECD jurisdictions									
Hong Kong (China)	98.7	140.3	111.0	110.2	99.8	101.0	112.2	105.6	87.5
Indonesia	..	..	97.9	96.4	96.5	97.0	96.6	..	96.1
Liechtenstein	..	97.3	107.9	105.9	114.1	117.9	122.5	107.6	110.7

Note: For more details, please see the methodological notes in Annex C.
Source: OECD Global Pension Statistics.

StatLink https://stat.link/unmdeg

Rising equity valuations in 2023 contributed to the improvement of the funding position of DB plans. The gains that pension providers achieved on their equity holdings drove asset growth. These gains offset the negative impact of decreasing discount rates on the funding ratio, such as in the United States. By contrast, in Hong Kong (China) where pension providers achieved moderate investment gains in nominal terms in 2022, the actuarial position of DB plans worsened.

The indexation policy of benefits could have an impact on the evolution of the funding ratio of DB plans. For example, the funding ratio of DB plans in the Netherlands remained relatively stable in 2023, after improvements in 2021 and 2022. The improvement of the funding ratio slowed down as pension funds to some extent granted higher benefits indexed to inflation to some pensioners.[4]

Any entry or exit from the sample of DB plans can also influence the evolution of the funding ratio calculated at the aggregated level. For example, a large decline in the aggregated funding ratio happened in Iceland between 2016 and 2017 due to the conversion of a public-sector scheme for state and municipal employees (one with the highest funding ratio) into a DC plan, therefore leaving the sample of DB plans on which the aggregated funding ratio is calculated.

4.3. The shift away from defined benefit plans continued despite improvements in funding ratios

The shift away from DB plans continued despite the improvement of the funding ratio in 2022 and 2023 in most jurisdictions. The share of assets in DB plans declined in all reporting jurisdictions in 2023 except Finland where DB plans continued to account for around 90% or more of assets (Figure 4.2).

Figure 4.2. Share of assets in defined benefit plans in selected jurisdictions, 2001-2023

As a percentage of total assets earmarked for retirement (excluding reserves of unfunded/PAYG plans)

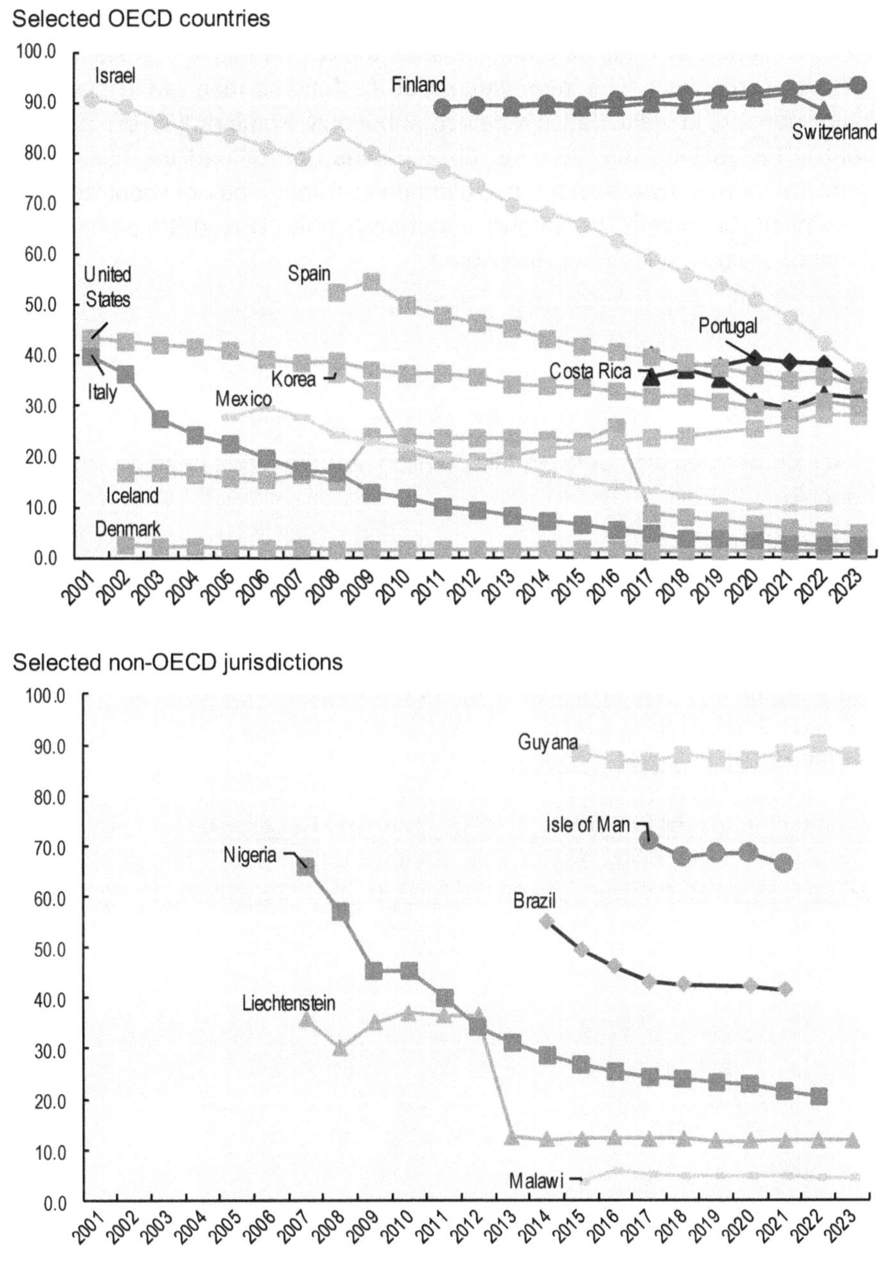

Source: OECD Global Pension Statistics.

StatLink https://stat.link/yoht3l

The long-term shift away from DB plans has several reasons. Employers are usually responsible for covering any funding shortfall in the case of traditional DB plans. The fall in interest rates over the years has made the promise of DB plans harder to meet (OECD, 2015[18]) and has led some employers to close their DB plans and offer DC plans instead (OECD, 2016[19]). The move to DC plans also makes contributions to the plan more predictable, which is one of the reasons employers moved away from DB plans in the United States, for example.[5] In some other cases, countries legislated the closure of some DB schemes to new entrants. For example, a 1993 legislative decree in Italy closed existing DB plans for specific sectors (e.g. banking sector) to new members and introduced supplementary DC pension plans for all. Israel also closed access to DB plans and granted access to DC plans to the whole population in 1995.

The shift away from DB plans continues as sponsors seek the opportunity to transfer their liabilities while the solvency of DB plans improves. The improvement of the funding ratio of DB plans alleviated some pressure on the plan sponsors to make deficit repair contributions. Some employers are taking advantage of the improvement in the funding ratio to wind up schemes and offload the risks and liabilities. For example, the amount transferred away to insurance companies through buy-out contracts reached a record level in 2023 in the United Kingdom.[6] The amount transferred in the United States fell in 2023 compared to 2022, but the number of buy-out contracts increased.[7]

Notes

[1] This section focuses on pension providers. Public pension reserve funds have no specific obligation to a specific group of people.

[2] COVID-19 has had a significant short-term impact on mortality rates and life expectancy (OECD, 2023[21]).

[3] Data for the United Kingdom are at end-March 2023.

[4] Dutch pension sector's funding ratio improves in third quarter 2023 | De Nederlandsche Bank (dnb.nl)

[5] Private Pension Plan Bulletin - Cover (dol.gov)

[6] Buy-ins and buy-outs hit a record £50 billion in 2023 - Hymans Robertson

[7] U.S. pension risk transfer sales premium increased 53% in Q4 2023: report | Benefits Canada.com

References

AP6 (2024), *Annual Report 2023*, https://www.ap6.se/en/documents/annual-report/. [4]

BIS (2024), *BIS Quarterly Review, March 2024*, https://www.bis.org/publ/qtrpdf/r_qt2403a.pdf. [3]

FRR (Annual Report 2023), *2024*, https://www.fondsdereserve.fr/documents/FRR-RA2023-EN.pdf. [10]

ILO (2024), *World Employment and Social Outlook - Trends 2024*, https://doi.org/10.54394/HQAE1085. [7]

IMF (2024), *Global Financial Stability Report: The Last Mile: Financial Vulnerabilities and Risks.* [2]

Mesa-Lago, C. (2021), *Evaluation of Four Decades of Pension Privatization in Latin America,1980-2020: Promises and reality.* [13]

Milliman (2024), *Pension Funding Index January 2024*, https://www.milliman.com/en/insight/pension-funding-index-january-2024. [17]

Ministry for Inclusion, Social Security and Migration (2024), *Reserve fund a report to the Parliament - Developments, actions in 2023 and status as of 31 December 2023.* [11]

OECD (2024), *Annual Survey of Investment Regulation of Pension Providers 2024.* [16]

OECD (2024), *OECD Employment Outlook 2024: The Net-Zero Transition and the Labour Market*, OECD Publishing, https://doi.org/10.1787/ac8b3538-en. [6]

OECD (2023), *Annual survey on financial incentives for retirement savings*, https://www.oecd.org/content/dam/oecd/en/publications/reports/2023/12/annual-survey-on-financial-incentives-for-retirement-savings_cc411907/2154cc08-en.pdf. [5]

OECD (2023), *Mortality and the Provision of Retirement Income*, OECD Publishing, https://doi.org/10.1787/a10a6c09-en. [21]

OECD (2023), *Pension Markets in Focus 2023*, OECD Publishing, https://doi.org/10.1787/28970baf-en. [12]

OECD (2023), *Pensions at a Glance 2023: OECD and G20 Indicators*, OECD Publishing, https://doi.org/10.1787/678055dd-en. [22]

OECD (2022), *OECD Reviews of Pension Systems: Korea, OECD Reviews of Pension Systems*, OECD Publishing, https://doi.org/10.1787/2f1643f9-en. [15]

OECD (2021), *Pension Markets in Focus 2021*, https://doi.org/10.1787/a70e4160-en. [9]

OECD (2019), *Pensions at a Glance 2019: OECD and G20 Indicators*, OECD Publishing, https://doi.org/10.1787/b6d3dcfc-en. [8]

OECD (2016), *OECD Pensions Outlook 2016*, OECD Publishing, https://doi.org/10.1787/pens_outlook-2016-en. [19]

OECD (2015), *OECD Business and Finance Outlook 2015*, OECD Publishing, https://doi.org/10.1787/9789264234291-en. [18]

OECD (forthcoming), *OECD Pensions Outlook 2024*, OECD Publishing, https://doi.org/10.1787/51510909-en. [23]

PPI (2024), *Pension scheme assets – a deep dive into alternatives*, https://www.pensionspolicyinstitute.org.uk/media/ugen4wez/20240916-deep-dive-1.pdf. [14]

SFC (2024), *Research Paper No.74: A Review of the Global and Local Securities Markets in 2023*, https://www.sfc.hk/-/media/EN/files/SOM/RS-Paper/RS-paper-74.pdf?rev=1fe5ffe6d12f4265a291367ea27242c9&hash=FDBF47FC1777BC217D4E2C3DA99EF97F. [1]

Stewart, F. and J. Yermo (2008), "Pension Fund Governance: Challenges and Potential Solutions", *OECD Working Papers on Insurance and Private Pensions*, No. 18, OECD Publishing, Paris, https://doi.org/10.1787/241402256531. [20]

Annex A. Features of asset-backed pension systems

Asset-backed pension systems include various types of arrangements around the world. These arrangements finance the benefits of retirees in different ways, through specific vehicles administered by different entities acting as pension providers (Figure A A.1). The way individuals get access to these arrangements and the type of benefits offered also vary across jurisdictions.

Figure A A.1. Features of asset-backed pension arrangements and evolution of the scope of Pension Markets in Focus

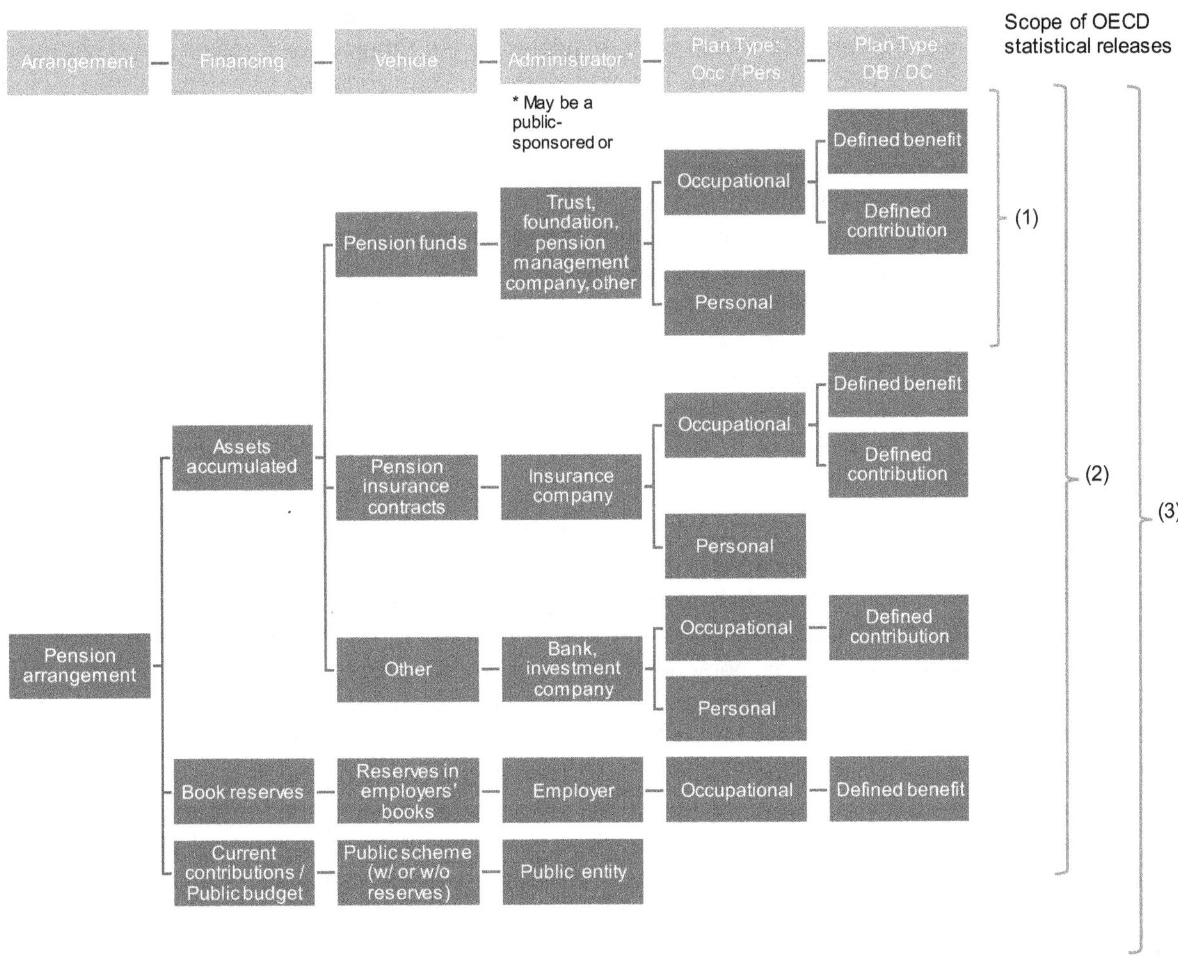

Note: For more details, please see the methodological notes in Annex C.

StatLink https://stat.link/tzna9w

Pension arrangements are designed to provide benefits to individuals at retirement but finance these benefits in various ways. Benefits can be financed through assets accumulated, through provisions in employers' books, from current contributions or from the public budget.

Members can accrue rights or accumulate assets for their retirement through their contributions or the contributions of their employers during their working lives. These assets are legally separated from the sponsors of the pension plans. Members have a legal or beneficial right or some other contractual claim on these assets.

By contrast, provisions in employers' books are not legally separated from the employers. The accrued pension rights of employees could potentially be at risk if the employers go bankrupt. Some countries where this financing method exists have set up insolvency guarantee schemes (e.g. Germany). Other countries encourage or require employers to purchase credit insurance or arrange equivalent guarantees (e.g. Sweden) to protect the pension rights of employees in the event of employer insolvency.

In most countries, the current contributions that employees and employers pay into public pension arrangements are used to pay the benefits of current retirees (i.e. unfunded or pay-as-you-go (PAYG) plans), while in some others retirement income may be financed by tax revenues (e.g. some social assistance programmes). These arrangements are usually administered by a public institution and may have reserves to cover expenses and smooth benefit payments over time.

Some pension arrangements rely both on current contributions and assets accumulated to finance benefits, such as the earning-related pension plans regulated by the Employees' Pension Act (TyEL) and the Seafarer's Pensions Act (MEL) in Finland. The main part of the pensions in a given year is paid by the contributions received that year. The remaining part is financed by accumulated assets.

Pension plans may be funded through the establishment of pension funds, pension insurance contracts or the purchase of other authorised retirement savings products. Pension funds represent a pool of ring-fenced assets forming an independent legal entity. When pension insurance contracts are used for retirement saving, individuals or their employers pay premiums to insurance companies. Insurance companies manage the assets coming from these premiums (or contributions) together with those coming from their other insurance activities. While the amount of premiums paid for these policies is usually known, it is more difficult to assess the size of assets that insurance companies hold as a result of their pension activities. Individuals or their employers may also open or purchase other retirement savings products offered and administered by banks or investment companies (such as individual retirement accounts (IRAs) in the United States).

Pension funds take different legal forms around the world (Stewart and Yermo, 2008[20]). Pension funds may have a legal personality and capacity in some countries (e.g. Pensionskassen in Austria and Germany, contractual pension funds in Italy, pension funds in the Netherlands and Switzerland). Pension funds in these countries have their own governing board. In some other countries, pension funds are segregated pools of assets without legal personality and capacity. In this case, pension funds are governed and administered by a separate entity. This entity may be a pension fund management company (e.g. in Czechia, Chile, Mexico, the Slovak Republic), a bank or an insurance company for instance. In some other countries (e.g. Ireland, the United Kingdom), the legal form of the pension fund is a trust. The trustees legally own and administer the assets of the trust in the interest of plan members. Irrespective of the legal form of the pension funds, some of the activities, such as those related to the investment of assets or the collection of contributions, may be outsourced to third parties (e.g. asset managers).

Employers (from the public or private sector) may set up a pension plan on behalf of their employees. In such cases, the plan is considered as occupational in the OECD taxonomy.[1] Access to the plan is linked to employment. When individuals choose and set up a plan themselves with a dedicated provider, the plan is personal. Access to certain plans may however be limited to individuals with a professional activity but open to both public and private sector workers (e.g. Mexico). These plans are still considered as personal as individuals independently select material aspects of the plan such as the investment strategy, the fund or the administrator of the fund.

Where the employer is responsible for guaranteeing a benefit or return promise to plan members, the OECD classified such occupational plan as a defined benefit (DB) plan.[2] The benefit promise may be a pension calculated on a number of parameters (e.g. salary, length of employment) or an investment rate of return. In the first case, the plan is considered as DB traditional, while the plan is considered as DB hybrid in the second case. When another party offers a guarantee (e.g. an insurance company), the plan is considered as a protected defined contribution (DC) plan. Otherwise, if there is no (fixed) guarantee, the plan is DC unprotected.

The Global Pension Statistics (GPS) exercise that the OECD carries out in co-operation with the IOPS and the World Bank covers employers' book reserves (which are private pension plans) and all plans accumulating assets, regardless of the financing vehicle and its administrator (public or private institution), the type of plans (occupational, personal, DB or DC) and the type of people covered (public sector workers, private sector workers). Unfunded or pay-as-you-go arrangements with their reserves are out of the scope of this exercise.

This publication mainly relies on the data collected through this statistical exercise. It endeavours to show data for all plans accumulating assets (funded plans) and book reserves, since the 2017 edition of this annual report (scope (2) in Figure A A.1).

Data in the GPS exercise – and therefore in this report – may not always cover book reserves and all plans accumulating assets that exist in each country due to data availability issues. Data are sometimes unavailable ("missing") for a given type of plan in a country (e.g. book reserves in Austria). In other cases, data may be missing only for some plans in a given type of plan. In Ireland for example, two plans qualify as pension insurance contracts according to the OECD taxonomy: retirement annuity contracts and personal retirement savings accounts (PRSAs). Data in the GPS exercise only cover PRSAs. Table A A.1 shows the types of pension plans and book reserves that exist in all the jurisdictions participating in the OECD, IOPS and World Bank statistical exercise. The table also specifies the coverage of the OECD data. More information is available online on the different pension plans in each jurisdiction.[3]

Pension Markets in Focus has benefitted from a broader coverage of asset-backed pension systems since the 2023 edition, through the incorporation of reserves of public PAYG pension arrangements in the OECD area (scope (3) in Figure A A.1). Data on these public reserves mainly come from the website of the public pension reserve funds managing these reserves and from desk research.

Table A A.1. Existing types of asset-backed pension plans and book reserves by jurisdictions and data coverage of the Global Pension Statistics exercise

	Funded								Book reserves
	Pension funds			Pension insurance contracts			Other		
	Occupational		Personal	Occupational		Personal	Occupational	Personal	
	DB	DC		DB	DC				
OECD countries									
Australia	✓	✓	✓					**Some**	
Austria	**Some**	✓		✓	**Some**	**Some**			Missing
Belgium	✓	✓	**Some**	✓	✓	✓		**Some**	
Canada	✓	✓	**Some**	✓	✓	✓		**Some**	✓
Chile		✓	✓		Missing	Missing	Missing	Missing	
Colombia			✓						
Costa Rica	✓	✓	✓						
Czechia			✓						
Denmark	✓		✓		✓	✓	✓	✓	

	Funded								Book reserves
	Pension funds			Pension insurance contracts			Other		
	Occupational		Personal	Occupational		Personal	Occupational	Personal	
	DB	DC		DB	DC				
Estonia			✓			✓			
Finland	✓			✓		✓			Missing
France	✓	✓	✓	✓	✓	✓			
Germany	✓	✓		Missing	Missing	Missing		Missing	Missing
Greece		✓				Missing			
Hungary		Missing	✓			✓		✓	
Iceland	✓	✓	✓			✓		✓	
Ireland	✓	✓				***Some***		✓	
Israel	✓		✓			Missing		***Some***	
Italy	✓	✓	✓			✓			✓
Japan	✓	✓	✓			✓			✓
Korea				✓	✓	✓	✓	✓	
Latvia		✓	✓					✓	
Lithuania			✓						
Luxembourg	✓	✓			Missing	Missing		Missing	Missing
Mexico	✓	✓	✓	✓	✓	Missing	✓	Missing	
Netherlands	✓	✓		Missing	Missing	Missing			
New Zealand	✓	✓	✓					✓	
Norway	✓			✓	✓	✓			
Poland		✓	✓		✓	✓	✓	✓	
Portugal	✓	✓	✓	Missing	Missing	✓		✓	
Slovak Republic			✓						
Slovenia		✓	✓		✓	✓			
Spain	✓	✓	✓	✓	✓	✓			✓
Sweden	✓	✓	✓	✓	✓	***Some***		✓	***Some***
Switzerland	✓					✓		✓	
Türkiye	Some	✓	✓						✓
United Kingdom	✓	✓		Missing	Missing	Missing			
United States	✓	✓				✓		✓	
Other jurisdictions									
Albania		✓	✓						
Angola	✓	✓							
Armenia			***Some***						
Botswana		✓	✓						
Brazil	✓	✓				✓			
Bulgaria		✓	✓						
Croatia		✓	✓						
Dominican Republic	✓	***Some***	✓						
Egypt	✓	✓							
Georgia			✓			✓			
Ghana		✓	✓						
Gibraltar				✓	✓	Missing	✓		
Guyana	✓	✓							
Hong Kong (China)	✓	✓		✓	✓				
India	***Some***	✓	✓						
Indonesia	✓	✓	✓						
Isle of Man	✓	✓	✓						
Jamaica	✓	✓	✓						
Kazakhstan			✓						
Kenya	✓	✓	✓						
Kosovo*		✓							
Lesotho	✓	✓	Missing						

	Funded								Book reserves
	Pension funds			Pension insurance contracts			Other		
	Occupational		Personal	Occupational		Personal	Occupational	Personal	
	DB	DC		DB	DC				
Liechtenstein	✓	✓							
Macau (China)	✓	✓	✓						
Malawi	✓	✓							
Malaysia	Missing		✓			✓			
Maldives			✓						
Malta		✓	✓			✓			
Mauritius	✓	✓	Missing			Missing			
Morocco		✓							
Mozambique	✓	✓							
Namibia	✓	✓	✓			✓			
Nigeria	✓		✓						
North Macedonia		✓	✓						
Pakistan	Missing	Missing	✓						
Peru			✓						
Romania			✓						
Serbia		✓	✓						
South Africa	✓	✓	✓				✓	✓	
Suriname	✓	✓			Missing	Missing			
Tanzania	***Some***		✓						
Thailand		***Some***	Missing						
Uganda	✓	✓	✓						
Ukraine			✓						
Uruguay			✓						
Zambia	***Some***	✓	Missing			Missing			
Zimbabwe	***Some***	✓	Missing			Missing			

Note: "DB": defined benefit; "DC": defined contribution. This Table gives the data coverage of this report, based on the OECD Global Pension Statistics (GPS) exercise. When a cell has a tick, this means that the GPS exercise covers all the plans of this type for a given country. "Some" means that the GPS exercise only covers some plans of this type. "Missing" means that this type of plan exists but the OECD data do not cover it. Data for Australia cover the whole superannuation sector except retirement savings accounts. Data for Germany refer to Pensionskassen and Pensionsfonds only. In Hungary, there is one institution for occupational retirement provision but its market share is negligible compared to other pension providers administering personal pension plans and its winding up has begun in 2024. In Norway, since 2021, members of DC schemes can consolidate their previous DC savings and contributions from their current job into a single account (own pension account). See Table A B.2 for a full and detailed description of all types of funded plans and book reserves in the jurisdictions participating in the OECD GPS exercise. Any deviation to this data coverage in this report is reported in the specific notes of the related Table or Figure.
* This designation is without prejudice to positions on status, and is in line with United Nations Security Council Resolution 1244/99 and the Advisory Opinion of the International Court of Justice on Kosovo's declaration of independence.

StatLink https://stat.link/wqf2n6

Annex B. Statistical annex

Table A B.1. Additional statistical tables

Table B.1. Total assets of pension providers, in millions of national currency, 2001-2023
Table B.2. Total assets of pension providers, in USD million, 2001-2023
Table B.3. Total assets of pension providers, as a % of GDP, 2001-2023
Table B.4. Contributions to pension providers, 2001-2023
Table B.5. Pension benefit flows, 2001-2023
Table B.6. Annual nominal investment rates of return of pension providers, 2002-2023
Table B.7. Annual real investment rates of return of pension providers, 2002-2023
Table B.8. Allocation of assets of pension providers in equities, 2001-2023
Table B.9. Allocation of assets of pension providers in bills and bonds, 2001-2023
Table B.10. Allocation of assets of pension providers in cash and deposits, 2001-2023
Table B.11. Allocation of assets of pension providers in the "other" category, 2001-2023
Table B.12. Share of assets of pension providers invested abroad, 2001-2023
Table B.13. Evolution in the participation rate, by type of plan

StatLink https://stat.link/pt0x6b

Table A B.2. Overview of asset-backed pension systems

Table B.14. Coverage of the OECD Global Pension Statistics exercise

StatLink https://stat.link/r9fqet

Annex C. Methodological notes

Pension authorities and other bodies provided the primary source material for this report, as part of the OECD/IOPS/ World Bank Global Pension Statistics (GPS) exercise. Data come from official administrative sources and are revised on an ongoing basis so as to better reflect the most recent figures for every past year. Some divergences may exist between national reporting standards and the compilation method of certain data for the GPS exercise. For this reason, data providers are regularly requested to provide methodological information relevant for developing a thorough understanding of their submission under the GPS framework. The general and specific methodological notes below provide some explanations in this respect.

General notes

- Conventional signs: ".." means not available. "|" means methodological break in series.
- This report is mainly based on the answers of pension authorities and other bodies to an annual data request. Some statistics for some jurisdictions come from publicly available reports, databases or websites of other national or international organisations: Japan (Bank of Japan) and Switzerland (Federal Social Insurance Office's publication *Statistique des assurances sociales suisses* for personal plans) among OECD countries; and Argentina (International Association of Pension Fund Supervisors (AIOS)), Bolivia (AIOS), China (People's Republic of) (Ministry of Human Resources and Social Security (MOHRSS)), Croatia (website of the Croatian Financial Services Supervisory Agency (HANFA) before 2014), the Dominican Republic (AIOS before 2014), El Salvador (AIOS), India (annual reports of the Employees' Provident Fund Organisation for Employees' Provident Fund, Employees' Pension Scheme and Employees' Deposit Linked Insurance Scheme), Panama (AIOS) and Uruguay (AIOS before 2016) among non-OECD jurisdictions.
- Data on stock variables refer to the end of the year while data on flow variables are provided over the whole year in the report. The reference period is the calendar year, except for: Australia where the reference period is the financial year ending in June; India where the reference period ends in March of the following year for Employees' Provident Fund, Employees' Pension Scheme and Employees' Deposit Linked Insurance Scheme; and New Zealand (until 2014). Data for New Zealand up to 2013 are based on a 31 March balance date for most of the schemes.
- Slovenia adopted the euro in 2007, the Slovak Republic in 2009, Estonia in 2011, Latvia in 2014, Lithuania in 2015 and Croatia in 2023. The whole time series (in millions of national currency) are expressed in millions of euros for these countries (even before their adoption of the euro).
- This report uses four main additional reference series: exchange rates to convert values in US dollars, GDP, the variation of the consumer price index (CPI) and population:
    - This report uses end-of-period exchange rates for all variables valued at the end of the year, and period-average rates for variables representing a flow over the year. These rates mainly come from the OECD Annual Purchasing Power Parities and Exchange Rates and the IMF International Financial Statistics databases.
    - GDP values come from the OECD Annual and Quarterly National Accounts databases for OECD countries; and from the IMF World Economic Outlook released in April 2024 for all the

other jurisdictions except Gibraltar (Abstract of Statistics 2015 of the Statistics Office of Gibraltar), Isle of Man (the National Income webpage of the Official Isle of Man Government website) and Liechtenstein (UN National Accounts Main Aggregates Database).

- Consumer price indices are from the OECD Consumer Price Indices database or from the IMF International Financial Statistics database except for Albania in 2023 (IMF World Economic Outlook of April 2024), Gibraltar (Abstract of Statistics 2015 of the Statistics Office of Gibraltar), Malawi in 2023 (IMF World Economic Outlook of April 2024), Papua New Guinea (World Bank Consumer Price Index database) and Suriname in 2023 (IMF World Economic Outlook of April 2024).
- Data on population are from the OECD Working-age Population database and World Bank World Development Indicators.

Specific notes

Figure 1.1:

This chart shows the amount of assets in all OECD pension providers and public pension reserve funds (PPRFs) for which data are available in a given year. It covers a few more PPRFs in 2022 than in 2023 but their size is small relative to the total assets (less than 5% of total assets in PPRFs).

Figure 1.2:

The charts show the nominal growth rates of assets of pension providers (Panel A) and public pension reserve funds (Panel B) expressed in national currency. Data for public pension reserve funds refer to: Future Fund for Australia; the reserves of Canada Pension Plan (CPP) and Quebec Pension Plan (QPP) for Canada; Pension Reserve Fund (PRF) for Chile; the Social Security Fund for Costa Rica; Keva and the State Pension Fund (VER) for Finland; AGIRC-ARRCO and Fonds de Réserves pour les Retraites (FRR) for France; National Insurance Fund (NIF) for Israel; Government Pension Investment Fund (GPIF) for Japan; National Pension Fund (NPF) for Korea; Fonds de Compensation (FDC) for Luxembourg; the Labour Fund for Mexico; the New Zealand (NZ) Superannuation Fund for New Zealand; the Government Pension Fund - Norway (GPFN) for Norway; Demographic Reserve Fund (DRF) for Poland; the Social Security Financial Stabilisation Fund (FEFSS) for Portugal; the Social Security Reserve Fund (SSRF) for Spain; AP1-AP4 and AP6 for Sweden; the AHV Central Compensation Fund for Switzerland; the Old-Age and Survivors Insurance (OASI) Trust Fund for the United States. (1) Data refer to pension funds only.

Figure 1.3:

Data for public pension reserve funds refer to: Future Fund for Australia; the reserves of Canada Pension Plan (CPP) and Quebec Pension Plan (QPP) for Canada; Pension Reserve Fund (PRF) for Chile; the Social Security Fund for Costa Rica; Keva and the State Pension Fund (VER) for Finland; AGIRC-ARRCO, Fonds de Réserves pour les Retraites (FRR) and the reserves of special regimes for France; National Insurance Fund (NIF) for Israel; Government Pension Investment Fund (GPIF) for Japan; National Pension Fund (NPF) for Korea; Fonds de Compensation (FDC) for Luxembourg; the Labour Fund for Mexico; the New Zealand (NZ) Superannuation Fund for New Zealand; the Government Pension Fund - Norway (GPFN) for Norway; Demographic Reserve Fund (DRF) for Poland; the Social Security Financial Stabilisation Fund (FEFSS) for Portugal; the Social Security Reserve Fund (SSRF) for Spain; AP1-AP4 and AP6 for Sweden; the AHV Central Compensation Fund for Switzerland; the Old-Age and Survivors Insurance (OASI) Trust Fund for the United States.

Figure 1.4:

This chart shows the nominal growth rates of assets of pension providers expressed in national currency. (1) Data cover voluntary plans only.

Figure 1.6:

The charts are based on the annual investment rates of return reported in the statistical annex of the report. Please refer to the notes of this statistical annex for more country or fund-specific notes. The annual returns are calculated over the period December 2022-December 2023 except for: pension providers in Australia (June 2022-June 2023); and Canada's CPP reserves (March 2023-March 2024), Japan's GPIF (March 2023-March 2024), New Zealand Superannuation Fund (June 2022-June 2023).

Figure 1.7:

The "Other" category includes loans, land and buildings, unallocated insurance contracts, hedge funds, private equity funds, structured products, other mutual funds (i.e. not invested in equities, bills and bonds or cash and deposits) and other investments. Negative values (due to derivatives) have been excluded from the calculations of the allocation of pension assets. The Global Pension Statistics exercise gathers information on investments of pension plan assets in collective investment schemes (CIS) and the look-through of these investments in equities, bills and bonds, cash and deposits and other. Data on asset allocation in this Figure include both direct investments in equities, bills and bonds, cash and deposits and indirect investments through CIS when the look-through of CIS investments is available. In such case, the Figure shows the overall exposure of pension plan assets in the selected asset classes. When the look-through is not available, the Figure only shows the direct investments of pension plan assets in equities, bills and bonds, cash and deposits and other assets, and investments in collective investment schemes are shown in a separate category.

Figure 1.8:

(1) Data refer to the second pension pillar. (2) Data refer to occupational pension plans only. (3) Data refer to personal pension plans only. (4) Data refer to pension funds only. (5) The excess of contributions over expenditure is calculated as the difference between contributions and the sum of benefits and operating expenses. (6) Data refer to pension funds and book reserves only. (7) Data refer to NPS and APY schemes. (8) Data refer to voluntary plans only.

Figure 2.2:

Other PPRFs include Canada's reserve of the Quebec Pension Plan, Chile's Pension Reserve Fund, the Costa Rican Social Security Fund, Finland's Keva, Finland's State Pension Fund, France's AGIRC-ARRCO (2022-2023 only), France's Fonds de Réserves pour les Retraites, France's reserves of special regimes (2023 only), Germany's Sustainability Fund (2021-2022 only), Israel's National Insurance Fund, Italy's Privatised funds under L.D 509/1994 and L.D 103/1996 (2021-2022 only), Korea's Government Employees Pension Fund (2021-2022 only), Luxembourg's Fonds de Compensation, Mexico's Labour Fund, New Zealand Superannuation Fund, the Government Pension Fund - Norway (GPFN), Poland's Demographic Reserve Fund, Portugal's Social Security Financial Stabilisation Fund, Spain's Social Security Reserve Fund, Switzerland's AHV Central Compensation Fund and the UK's National Insurance Fund (2021-2022 only). The difference in PPRFs covered in the "other PPRFs" may distort the trend marginally.

Figure 2.3:

The percent change of assets is calculated as the difference between the value of assets at end-2023 and at end-2021 over the value of assets at end-2021 in USD. The charts show the results of the calculations based on values in USD on the x-axis, and those based on values in national currency on the y-axis. The results are not shown for Türkiye (36.9% based on USD values, 210.5% based on values in national currency) nor for Spain's PPRF (154.6% in USD values, 160.9% in national currency) for readability purposes.

Figure 2.4:

The charts show the level of assets at end-2022 and at end-2023 relative to end-2021 (the reference, set at 100%). A level at 90 relative to 100 indicates a 10% decline in assets. By contrast, a level at 110 indicates a 10% increase in assets. The levels for Türkiye are not shown for readability purposes (179.1% at end-2022 and 310.5 at end-2023). The level at end-2023 is not shown for Georgia (222.2%) nor for Spain's Social Security Reserve Fund (260.9%) for readability purposes. (1) Data cover voluntary plans only.

Figure 2.5:

The charts show the nominal investment rates of return (IRRs) in 2022 (x-axis) and in 2023 (y-axis). The curve shows the break-even rate: the investment gains (resp. losses) to record the following year to fully offset the losses (resp. lose the gains) of the previous year. Jurisdictions above the curve managed to record positive investment gains over the two years while those above recorded a loss. Pension providers in Türkiye recorded a nominal investment rate of return of 49.6% in 2022 and 46% in 2023, not shown for readability purposes.

Figure 2.6:

The excess of contributions over expenditure for 2022 is calculated as the difference between the change in assets between end-2021 and end-2022 and the investment income (net of investment expenses) earned during 2022. It is expressed as a percentage of assets at end-2021. Likewise, the excess of contributions over expenditure for 2022 and 2023 is calculated as the difference between the change in assets between end-2021 and end-2023 and the investment income (net of investment expenses) earned during 2022 and 2023. It is expressed as a percentage of assets at end-2021. Expenditure includes benefit payments to retirees, early withdrawals, administrative expenses and other operating expenses, and transfers out of the system. (1) Data cover voluntary plans only.

Figure 3.1:

The chart shows the amount of assets at the end of each year, from end-2001 to end-2023, based on annual data. The total amounts of assets at the end of a given year are calculated on all the jurisdictions and funds for which a value is available. The number of jurisdictions and funds that the totals include may therefore vary over the years. Totals are expressed in current prices.

Table 3.1:

(1) Data refer to pension funds only. (2) Data refer to personal pension plans only. (3) Data exclude ERAFP and CAVP. (4) Data cover closed and open pension funds and personal retirement saving funds (established as pension funds or as collective investment schemes managed by investment companies). (5) Data cover voluntary plans only.

Table 3.3:

(1) Data cover voluntary plans only.

Figure 3.2:

The average allocations of pension plan assets have been calculated over 15 jurisdictions: Austria, Czechia, Denmark, Germany, Japan, Netherlands, Norway, Poland, Slovenia (from 2003 onwards), Sweden, Türkiye (from 2004 onwards) and the United States among OECD countries; and Bulgaria, Hong Kong (China) (from 2002 onwards) and Peru among other jurisdictions. The whole time series of the asset allocation in each of these 15 jurisdictions are available in the statistical annex of this publication. The asset allocation of pension plans in 2019 in Korea and in 2011 in Türkiye are OECD estimates based on the data available for the year before and after the missing year.

Table 3.4:

The excess of contributions over expenditure for a given is calculated as the difference between the change in assets between the end of the given year and the previous one and the investment income (net of investment expenses) earned during that given year. The average annual excess of contributions over expenditure over a given number of years is calculated as the sum of the excess over these years divided by the number of years covered. The result is expressed as a percentage of total assets at end-2023. (1) Data cover voluntary plans only.

Figure 3.3:

The charts show the proportion of the working-age population participating in a pension arrangement at two different times: 1. the last year, which is the latest year from 2020 for which data is available; 2. the first year, which is the earliest date for which data is available. The first year is only shown if it is at least 5 years earlier than the last year (except when the type of plan was introduced within the 5 years). The first-year data refers to is shown as a label in blue, the last year in black.

A plan is classified as mandatory/quasi-mandatory, automatic enrolment, voluntary occupational or voluntary personal according to the way members access the plan in the last year shown. The access to the plan between the first and last year shown may have changed in some countries (e.g. Slovak Republic that introduced automatic enrolment in 2023).

See Annex B for the full time series and more specific notes on jurisdictions.

Figure 4.1:

The charts show the evolution of the liabilities (measured by the net technical provisions) of defined benefit (DB) plans at the end of each year. All liabilities of DB plans (instead of technical provisions only) are considered for Ireland and the United States. Data for Finland refer to DB plans in pension funds only. Data for Luxembourg refer to DB traditional plans under the supervision of the CSSF. Data for the Netherlands and Switzerland include all types of pension funds. Data for the United Kingdom come from the Purple Book 2023 published by the Pension Protection Fund and show the liabilities valued on an s179 basis (instead of net technical provisions). Liabilities for Hong Kong (China) refer to the amount of aggregated past service liability in DB ORSO schemes. Data for Indonesia cover DB EPFs only.

Table 4.1:

The funding ratio is calculated as the ratio of total investment and net technical provisions for DB plans managed by pension funds using values reported by national authorities in the OECD questionnaire. All liabilities of DB plans (instead of technical provisions only) are considered for Ireland and the United States. Data for Finland refer to DB plans in pension funds only. Data for Luxembourg refer to DB traditional plans under the supervision of the CSSF. Data for the Netherlands and Switzerland include all types of pension funds. Data for the United Kingdom come from the Purple Book 2023 published by the Pension Protection Fund and show the ratio of assets and liabilities valued on an s179 basis (instead of net technical provisions). Liabilities for Hong Kong (China) refer to the amount of aggregated past service liability in DB ORSO schemes. Data for Indonesia cover DB EPFs only.

Figure A A.1:

(1) Scope of the note Pension Funds in Figures (renamed Pension Markets in Focus - Preliminary data on pension funds) until 2022; and scope of the full report Pension Markets in Focus before the 2017 edition. (2) Scope of the OECD Global Pension Statistics exercise; scope of the note Pension Markets in Focus - Preliminary data since 2023; scope the full report Pension Markets in Focus since the 2017 edition until 2022. (3) Scope of Pension Markets in Focus since the 2023 edition.

Notes

[1] The definitions of pension plans by the OECD's Working Party on Private Pensions are available in the publication *Private Pensions: OECD Classification and Glossary*, available at https://www.oecd.org/daf/fin/private-pensions/privatepensionsoecdclassificationandglossary.htm.

[2] See https://www.oecd.org/daf/fin/private-pensions/privatepensionsoecdclassificationandglossary.htm.

[3] See https://www.oecd.org/pensions/private-pensions/pensionmarketsinfocus.htm

www.ingramcontent.com/pod-product-compliance
Lightning Source LLC
Chambersburg PA
CBHW061224240926
51846CB00006B/1350